MORE
WAIT WAIT ...
DON'T TELL ME!®
CROSSWORD PUZZLES

BY BRENDAN EMMETT QUIGLEY
AND CHRISTOPHER ADAMS
EDITED BY BENJAMIN TAUSIG

FOREWORD BY **PETER SAGAL**

CHRONICLE BOOKS
SAN FRANCISCO

ISBN: 978-1-7972-0204-4

Manufactured in China.

Designed by AJ Hansen and Tatiana Pavlova.

10 9 8 7 6 5 4 3 2 1

Chronicle Books LLC
680 Second Street
San Francisco, California 94107
www.chroniclebooks.com

INTRODUCTION

It's odd to think about how many amazing, unlikely, and downright gobsmackingly impossible things have happened since the first *Wait Wait . . . Don't Tell Me!* crossword puzzle book was published in 2014. For example, the perennial doormat Chicago Cubs won the World Series in 2016! Some other impossible things may have happened around then too, but generally, we were all too excited about the Cubs to notice.

More examples: in October of 2018, *Wait Wait . . . Don't Tell Me!* celebrated its 20th Anniversary on the air with a gala performance at the beautiful Chicago Theater in downtown . . . well, guess. We flew in almost all of our panelists, as well as NPR News titans Robert Siegel and Nina Totenberg, to celebrate by . . . well, by doing our show. We're generally amazed that you folks have allowed us to continue this long, and since we're not quite sure why, we're nervous of changing a thing. But we packed the place with 3,000 people, all of whom, we have learned, consider us friends, and believe me, we feel the same way about you.

We also suffered a profound loss, when our beloved original Judge and Scorekeeper, the soul of our show, Carl Kasell, passed away in the spring of 2018, just four years after he retired from the airwaves. Back when we began the show in 1998, it was Carl who let us coast on the affection he had earned over decades of broadcasting the news from NPR: if Carl Kasell was on the show, it couldn't be that bad, could it? (Spoiler: sometimes, it could.) Even in his absence, we are still inspired by the simple joy he took in performing our show, every week. He was wise enough to know that the attention of an audience is never to be squandered, never taken for granted, and always to be treasured. When I think of Carl, I think of just how much *fun* he had doing our show, and I'm able to put aside whatever trivial thing I might be annoyed by any given day, and realize that all of us at *Wait Wait* are, *pace* Lou Gehrig, the luckiest people on the face of the earth.

We continue to take joy in doing our show, making jokes about the week's news, even as the news has become both more alarming and outrageous, even as we're overwhelmed with real events that seem as if they were created by some demented scriptwriter. Some weeks are harder than others—we've often stared at each other in our offices in Chicago, saying, "How are we going to make *that* funny?"— but then we gather with Bill Kurtis and our panelists at our home theater in Chicago, or in some fabulous auditorium or performance center in a different city, and we convene a kind of séance, in which we manage to raise the spirits of the room. Many people have said to me, often at our regular meet and greets after our performances, that looking forward to our show helps them get through their week. I respond by telling them the truth: that being able to produce and perform the show for them helps us get through ours.

But perhaps the most amazing thing that's happened since the publication of Volume 1 is that I, Peter Sagal, have become a crossword puzzle nerd. Yes, I know: my foreword for the prior edition went on and on about how frustrating I found crosswords, how dumb they made me feel, etc., but then much to my astonishment, I was invited to provide color commentary at the 2016 American Crossword Puzzle Tournament in Stamford, CT. As I explained to my friend Greg Pliska, an experienced constructor and solver, and the man doing the "play by play," I don't understand crossword puzzles and have no idea how to talk about them. "It's not a problem," he said. "We don't either."

At the annual event—as immortalized in the 2006 documentary, *Wordplay*—hundreds of people come together to sit in a hotel banquet room and silently fill in grids of words. It's that exciting! And then, at the end, the finest solvers get up in front of everyone and fill in large grids printed on boards, while their vision is blocked from their competitors' grids, and their ears are blocked by headphones playing white noise, so they can't hear the announcers comment on their progress. It's nerd sports at its finest. And there I was, an outsider, trying to understand what was going on enough to say something interesting about it, if not actually amusing.

The puzzles were incomprehensible to me, as they always had been, and the exercise of filling them in seemed pointless, still. But the true revelation was the people—young and old, men and women, in a rainbow of colors and backgrounds, all devoted to this odd pastime, in which a small group of them drew up elaborate matrices of words, provided

obscure clues to the contents, and the rest of them filled them in. What was most shocking to me, at the time, was not their devotion to their hobby—the world is large, and filled with people pursuing odd pastimes—but the joy they got from doing it. They loved doing well. They appreciated being stymied. They loved trading clues and jokes and commentary on the puzzles, which varied in quality, but the fellowship never was anything less than superb.

In the end, that's what drew me in: not the challenge of the puzzles, but the quality of the people who were devoted to them. They were people I'd like to hang out with. In fact, given how kind, funny, witty, intellectual, humble, and simply joyful they all were as they went about their business of solving, they were the kind of people I wanted to be. So I started attempting the *New York Times* Crossword puzzle, the same puzzle that had so frustrated and humbled me decades before. First, of course, Monday through Wednesday, before it started to get really hard, but soon, as I practiced and learned, Thursdays, Fridays, and Saturdays as well. (I still don't really get into Sunday puzzles. They're just really long Wednesdays, and Wednesdays are long enough.)

As I wrote in the last edition, I thought of crossword puzzles as tests of my intelligence, and when I failed them, I took it as a judgment on me, one which I resented. But I have discovered, crosswords aren't so much a test as a lesson—in vocabulary, in creative thinking, in problem solving. One of my favorite things to do, now that I'm a daily solver, is to get stuck somewhere, not able to finish a grid . . . and then put it aside. I let my mind wander to other things, and then once I've let go of the brain-lock, come back to the puzzle, and see things I didn't see before. You let go of your preconceptions—say, the clue "Hunter in a movie" must be some kind of movie character who hunts—and then realize it's a reference to the actor, TAB. At my age, there is no greater pleasure than to learn, as Lincoln put it, to think anew.

In the fall of 2017, I even had the great pleasure of collaborating with constructor Mike Selinker on our own *New York Times* puzzle, and I discovered the joy of solving a puzzle was nothing compared to creating one. Because I finally knew how fun it was to pick apart the clues of context and language and spelling to fill in tricky grids, creating clues for others was like cooking a delicious meal for millions of friends at once. I may not be able to enjoy it myself, but I'd thrill to their anticipated delight. And, of course, their frustration—Lord knows it couldn't be too easy, because what's the fun of that?

So this, then, is perhaps the biggest difference between the first edition of *Wait Wait . . .* themed crosswords, and this one: I'm going to be solving this one along with you. I might have a bit of an advantage of course, because I know some of the moments from the show, and stories featured on it, that run through these puzzles . . . but on the other hand, don't be too sure. We've been doing this for more than twenty years. I'm a pretty old man, and I can't recall what I had for breakfast today, let alone what we said on the show in 2017. So it may be we'll start from the same place of ignorance and excitement.

Ready? We'll open the book and start the first puzzle on three. One, two . . . GO!

—PETER SAGAL, 2019

DOWN

1. Include in an email secretively
2. Yellowfin tuna
3. Japanese bread
4. Type of childhood complex
5. Old online newsgroup system
6. Medieval slave
7. Accra's country
8. Support
9. Hindu god of creation
10. Trucker's truck
11. Sound in "geese" but not in "giant"
12. Disney princess who wears a clam shell bra
13. Format for many a "Wait Wait…Don't Tell Me!" quiz
21. Scheduled soon
23. Van ___, CA
24. Haunted house resident
25. Variety show
26. Old-timey toothpaste
28. Country Time drink
31. Glass heard on NPR
33. Sweater's spot in a hotel?
36. "Let's talk price," in some classified listings
38. One-named Greek New Age musician
39. Manila folder feature
40. Poker Flat chronicler Bret
42. "I'm drowning here!"
43. Jacksonville NFL player, casually
46. Big start?
48. International service group founded in Detroit
50. Spanish-rice-and-seafood dish
52. Shoot for, with "to"
53. One of the black keys
54. Actress Witherspoon
55. "Maybe ___ crazy one?"
57. Give the slip to
60. For fear that
62. Store overhead, as on a plane
65. Nurse, as a beer
67. i or j part
68. Super Bowl XLII MVP Manning
69. Stimpy's cartoon bud

ACROSS

1. Marshy inlets of Louisiana
7. Talks on and on
11. Consumes
14. Ingredient in a melt
15. Put on staff
16. Notoriously hard-to-define thing
17. "This orangutan's heart is a ___…" (first line of a "Wait Wait…" limerick heard on February 4, 2017)
18. Garden of Eden guy
19. Brazilian metropolis
20. How some teasing is offered
22. "…An enclosure most romance does ___…" (second line of the limerick)
24. "…But I'm not one to…" (third line of the limerick)
27. Hand part
29. Hideous
30. Relating to the liver
32. Like shooting fish in a barrel
34. White House office shape
35. One of three accusations in the game of Clue
37. College lecture course topic, casually
41. Smiling orb in a child's picture of a garden, say
42. Orangutan at a Dutch zoo that uses 66-Across to find mates
44. ___ mode (covered with ice cream)
45. "I love you," from Juanita
47. Scottish island where Macbeth is buried
48. Bump on a log
49. "Get Up!" sports channel
51. Hostile to
53. Ship's prison
56. Became mature
58. "…I just sit, stare and ___…" (fourth line of the limerick)
59. Gender of 42-Across
61. Italian motor scooter maker
63. Give permission to
64. Disney princess who sings "Let It Go"
66. "…I'll find love with a smartphone and ___" (last line of the limerick)
70. Debris eliminated by e-cigarettes
71. Tried to beat the tag, maybe
72. Bird that lends its name to a baseball team
73. Merch table garment purchase, briefly
74. Merch table musical purchase
75. Big name in hotels

ACROSS

1. "Special counsel Robert Mueller said that hackers from ___ stole sensitive files in an effort to discredit the investigation"
7. "On Monday, The Justice Department unveiled charges against the Chinese tech giant ___"
13. Archipelago components
15. Went way out of control
16. Genre for artist Jasper Johns
17. "Golden Girls" name
18. Test for would-be PhDs
19. Isamu with a namesake table
21. Caddy beverage
22. "On Wednesday, the president of ___ warned that a U.S. invasion to remove him from power would lead to a war worse than Vietnam"
24. Ingested
26. Uses a swizzle stick, say
27. Getting things done, initially
30. Small hint
32. Alternatives to Ding Dongs
34. Take one's clothes off, again
37. Like silent letters
39. "On Tuesday, the Senate Judiciary Committee postponed the confirmation vote for William Barr, Trump's pick for ___"
41. "Moonstruck" Oscar winner
42. Resided, formally
43. Coin featuring FDR
44. Bit of ink, casually
45. Monetary consideration, for college students (or their parents)
47. Acapulco uncle
48. "On Wednesday, Senate Majority Leader Mitch McConnell railed against a bill that would make ___ a holiday"
51. Out of class
53. Connective tissue
56. ___ noire (pet peeve)
57. Cheri formerly of SNL
61. Like a rock
62. Rival of Schmeling
63. With 66-Across, "On Tuesday, longtime Trump adviser ___ pled not guilty to allegations that he lied to investigators"
64. "Cunning hunter" of the Bible
65. Airport postings, for short
66. See 63-Across
67. Hawaiian state bird

DOWN

1. Phone call sound
2. Cause of many computer errors
3. Gin flavoring
4. In the dumps
5. Silly as can be
6. After-market accessories
7. Chops finely
8. Up to a point
9. Reverence
10. Droop, as flowers
11. Palindromic fashion magazine
12. Metaphorical light bulb
14. "Full House" actor Bob
15. Crop up again
20. Israeli weapon
22. It has direction and magnitude
23. Made up (for)
24. "Respect" singer Franklin
25. One sampling foodstuffs
28. One needing help
29. Ajax competitor whose name means "good friend" in French
30. Unit of land
31. Slip up
32. "Sugar pie" alternative
33. Canonized 5th-century pope
35. Circuit components that store energy in magnetic fields
36. Bird also known as a lapwing
37. ___ e olio (traditional pasta dish)
38. Cause to burn
40. Abominable mountain creature
45. Atomic number of neon
46. "Don't tell anyone" contract, for short
49. Looks maliciously
50. Pale as a ghost
51. "Mamma Mia!" quartet
52. "A 3-year-old who was lost in the woods for two days told his mom he survived because he was taken care of by a ___"
54. "On Wednesday, President Trump called his intelligence chiefs naive after they contradicted him on the dangers of ___"
55. For two, musically
58. Small child
59. Id companion
60. Kylo of "The Force Awakens"

ACROSS

1. After mastering kitesurfing, the "Wait Wait...Don't Tell Me!" panel predicted ___ would do the things in this puzzle's theme answers
6. Mexican peninsula
10. The fuzz or the heat
14. Like some warfare
15. Skipping base duties, say
16. Folkie Guthrie
17. Spin around
18. Schlep
19. NFL coach McVay
20. Cutlass automaker
21. With 26-Across, Peter Grosz said 1-Across would open a medical marijuana dispensary named ___
23. Ecological community
25. Makes less difficult
26. See 21-Across
29. With 44-Across, Mo Rocca said 1-Across would design one of these for 52-Across
31. Horoscope columnist Sydney
32. French pronoun used by Miss Piggy
33. General whose name is seen near beef and broccoli
36. Faith Salie said 1-Across would do synchronized ___ with 67-Across
41. ___ Nation (Jay-Z's entertainment company)
42. Increases
43. Like some sad keys
44. See 29-Across
46. Voicemail, e.g.
48. Like baklava and dolmadakia
51. Bordeaux wine region
52. See 29-Across
55. European capital serviced by Sandefjord Airport
59. "Clueless" phrase
60. Not every one wears a cape, it's said
61. Songwriters' org.
62. Torch that might hold citronella
63. Way off in the distance
64. Certain grave marker
65. Scorch, as a steak
66. Cunning
67. Infamous foreign president

DOWN

1. "I'm ___ you!"
2. Cry like a baby
3. Extremely enthusiastic
4. Chocolate candies with nougat
5. The whole shooting match
6. Grand ___ Island
7. Fully cognizant
8. Soup du ___
9. One on your side
10. "Rock the ___" (Clash hit)
11. Cookies crumbled into ice cream
12. Wood shop tool
13. Spotify selections
21. Guitarist Scaggs
22. Hardened
24. Memo subject heading letters
26. 1922 physics Nobelist Niels
27. The Herman Melville book you'd think was more popular than "Moby Dick" if you only did crosswords
28. Drug capturer
29. ___ choy
30. Stuff from a gas station pump
32. Hammer and Lyte
33. Beyoncé and Solange's mom
34. Kiss, to Prince William
35. Fairy tale bugbear
37. Mac
38. Close relative of a human
39. "___ Excited" (Pointer Sisters single)
40. "The Simpsons" character in a leisure suit
44. Colorful California tree
45. Approves
46. Kids' card game
47. Slate people: Abbr.
48. No-see-ums
49. Poster figure who says "We Can Do It!"
50. Eleniak of "Baywatch"
51. Aesopian lesson
53. Warming of snow, say
54. Bank offering, briefly
56. Shinty player
57. Legal scholar Guinier
58. Ready, as for business
61. Nile biter

ACROSS

1. Energetic conductor Seiji
6. Sharpen, as a blade
10. "We're done for!"
14. Golfer's warnings
15. "Nothing on my body is hurt"
16. ___ contendere (court plea)
17. "This week, French officials announced a ban on ___"
20. The Obama years, e.g.
21. Genesis garden
22. Talk show veteran O'Donnell
23. "After receiving a 911 call from a man complaining that he was too high, police in Ohio entered his apartment and found a man lying on the floor surrounded by ___"
25. Inclined
27. Taxpayer's ID fig.
28. Basketball, casually
29. "Tom's Diner" singer Suzanne
32. Dawn
33. School dance and bake sale gp.
36. "A Nebraska state senator is calling for a change to the design of the state flag after it was ___ over the state capitol for 10 days, and no one noticed"
40. One with a sharp tongue
41. Japanese port city
42. Ginger, e.g.
43. Sticky label company
44. Ad-Rock and Mike D's former bandmate
46. "Jeopardy!" questions
49. With 56-Across, "An Oklahoma man is being charged with a DUI after nearly running over people who were ___"
53. 1998 Disney princess
54. Type of singing club
55. Conservative or liberal leader?
56. See 49-Across
60. Abode that might be rolled up in the morning
61. English horn cousin
62. Seven, in Sonora
63. Really bothers
64. Creature in witches' brews
65. Praise to the hilt

DOWN

1. Eliminated, mob-style
2. Fictional swashbuckler
3. Toward the back
4. Tinier than teeny
5. Money in the bank, and so forth
6. Goes undercover
7. Sultan's nation
8. Either : or :: neither : ___
9. Stretch the budget, with "out"
10. Federations
11. English composer Gustav who composed "The Planets"
12. Skateboarding trick
13. Cleaned by shooting, with "down"
18. Get too high from
19. Sweet café offering
24. "___ what you did there …"
25. Justice Sotomayor
26. Garish, as some garments
28. Siberian dog
29. Ex-GIs' org.
30. Manning with Super Bowl rings
31. Captured
32. Practices in a ring
33. Toilet training verb
34. Snake eyes number
35. Little scurrier
37. Nine-day Catholic devotion
38. One agreeing to a software license
39. Small drink amount
43. Lies ahead
44. Outward expression
45. John of Monty Python
46. Stradivari's teacher
47. Wearing less clothes
48. Exited red-faced, with "away"
49. Bunch of ships
50. Map enlargement, often
51. "Wowee zowee!"
52. 1979 Douglas Hofstadter book "___, Escher, Bach"
54. Get taller
57. Made it to square 100 first in Chutes and Ladders, e.g.
58. Lincoln nickname
59. Highest number on dice, commonly

1	2	3	4	■	5	6	7	8	■	9	10	11	12	13
14				■	15				■	16				
17				■	18				■	19				
20				21				22		■	23			
■	■	■	24				■	25			26		■	■
■	27	28		29(○)			29					■	30	31
32			■	33				■	34					
35			36	■	37			38	39	■	40			
41				42	■	■	43			44	■	45		
46(○)					47	48					49			■
■	■	50				■	51				■	■	■	■
52	53		■	54			55				■	56	57(○)	58
59			60		■	61				■	62			
63				■	64				■	65			
66					■	67				■	68			

ACROSS

1. YouTube channel, say, in a modern portmanteau
5. Allure alternative
9. Like many IPAs
14. Photojournalist Robert
15. MGM mascot animal
16. Heart parts
17. Fancy hotel name
18. Rescue mission, briefly
19. Immune system agent
20. "This week, the nation turned its eyes to Lexington, Ky., where the Millcreek Elementary School staged its annual fourth-grade ___, which had a surprising winner. The panelists are each going to tell you who it was, but only one of them is telling the truth ..."
23. "Here's the thing ..."
24. "Life is ___ dream" ("Row, Row, Row Your Boat" line)
25. Exams for future docs
27. "The winner, 10-year-old Melissa Jeleno, unveiled her high-tech creation, an automated Twitter bot named Mean Girl. Melissa gave her hideous progeny a ___ and a flimsy bio and turned her loose on Twitter. Mean Girl's programming was simple. She'd reply to a random person's tweet with 1 of 200 mean but vague responses, like, "that's so offensive. You suck." Or, "why are you so triggered, snowflake?" Or "LOL, you are so stupid." If Mean Girl got a response, she was programmed to reply back with another insult, sometimes quoting her new enemy and adding "not" or "nuh-uh." Or "I am so totally reporting you. Bye-Bye." The goal was to see if any adults online would fall for her silly prank and get in a Twitter war with Mean Girl. As of last month, about 432,000 users have done just that."
32. Michelle of the LPGA
33. Fencing sword
34. 38th parallel peninsula
35. Beasts of burden
37. Grows nigh
40. Dice dots
41. Intensify
43. Trois squared
45. Kazan of "The Big Sick"
46. "Frank Miller, an 11-year-old scientist and student, took top prize for his invention, ___ —'Putting the Mmm in Metal Mouth.' Makes the sometimes painful, often uncomfortable rite of passage more appealing for kids. His catchphrase—'nobody wants braces on teeth. Everybody wants treats on teeth.' Might be clumsy but he's a child, remember, and it works. Using all-natural essences and oils, he successfully developed a number of flavored beta braces, including bubble gum–flavored train tracks and avocado-flavored retainers. Frank himself played guinea pig. His own preference is a combination of toffee and sea salt flavors."
50. Hawaiian island
51. Try again
52. "Elementary" actress Lucy
54. "Ten-year-old Ace Davis of Lexington won with his ambitious entry, 'Is Tom Brady a Cheater?' As Brady heads to his 67th Super Bowl thinking he was finally in the clear on the ___ controversy, he is faced with damning scientific evidence assembled by Davis that he did, in fact, gain a distinct advantage by de-inflating his footballs during the 2014 season. Davis had family members toss footballs filled with varying degrees of pressure to see which ones went the furthest. Test results proved incontrovertibly that low pressure in a football makes them fly further. Ace Davis now goes on to the Kentucky District Science Fair Finals while the disgraced Brady slinks off to Atlanta, Ga. and, no doubt, obscurity."
59. Legally old enough
61. Concluded, in Cannes
62. Without feeling
63. Last word of many fairy tales
64. "The Neverending Story" author Michael
65. Qatari, e.g.
66. Russian refusals
67. It's more, proverbially
68. Alternatives to bottles

DOWN

1. DVD players' predecessors
2. Of the flock
3. Prefix for vision-related words
4. Elegant garden pavilion
5. Important November event
6. Take on an assumed identity
7. Bakery purchase
8. Put down stakes?
9. Place for a pillbox, say
10. Without a prescription, briefly
11. Add air to, in a way
12. Shag carpet feature
13. New Haven school
21. "___ said!"
22. "Vous êtes ___" ("You are here," in French)
26. Convertible cousin
27. Screen resolution unit
28. Consider again
29. African antelope
30. Taken-back vehicles, casually
31. Lack of difficulty
32. Klingon in "Star Trek: The Next Generation"
36. ___ Ring (birth control option)
38. Changes one's marketing strategy, e.g.
39. Guarantees
42. Thinks over
44. Gradually disappear
47. "Party for One" singer Carly ___ Jepsen
48. Eponymous tower designer Gustave
49. Courvoisier, e.g.
52. Financial aid option
53. Debatable
55. Subway route
56. Distinct atmosphere
57. Eliot Ness, notably
58. Falls back, as the tide
60. Obtain

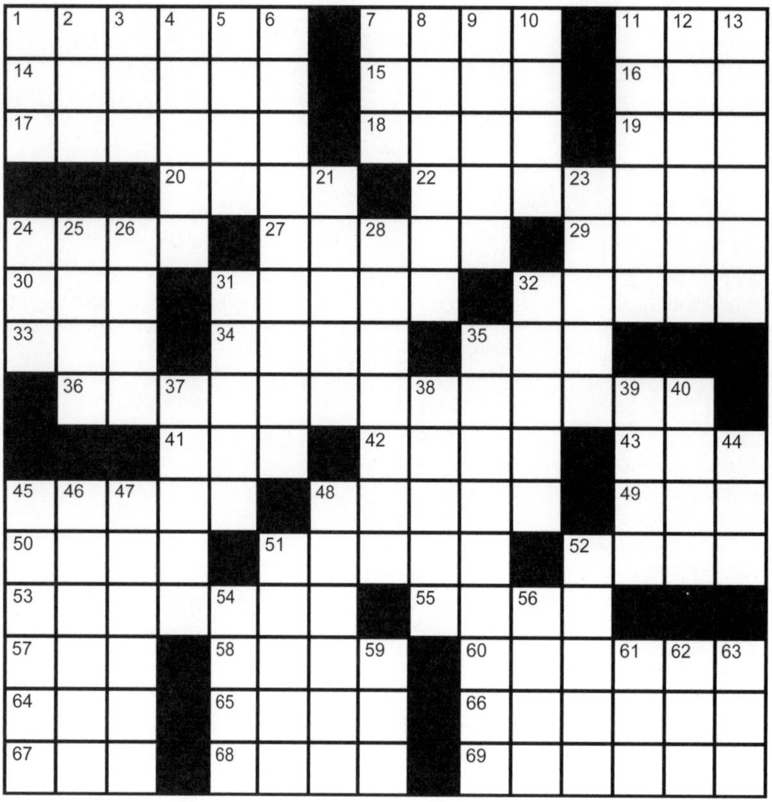

(Crossword grid with numbered cells)

4. "Bohemian Rhapsody" star Rami
5. Chichi
6. Take a bath, as a business on an investment
7. Pharaoh's snake
8. Standard-___ (leader)
9. Office program
10. Caustic cleaners
11. Overflowing with
12. Many
13. Greek peak of Thessaly
21. Deity of debauchery
23. Letter-shaped fastener
24. Hosts, as a roast
25. Literary captain of the Pequod
26. "Star Trek" helmsman
28. Square-shaped flier
31. NFL commissioner Goodell
32. Wrestling Hulk
35. Long, thin pasta type
37. Cold discharge
38. Lay to rest
39. Highest draft status
40. Thanksgiving tubers
44. Stir-fry pan
45. Observed Yom Kippur, in a way
46. Spreads news of
47. Typical
48. Words of (much-anticipated) relief
51. Started to pay attention
52. Act the troll
54. French cash
56. Best of the theater?
59. Stags and bucks and stallions, e.g.
61. Car park : UK :: ___ : US
62. Election Day day: Abbr.
63. Sex ed subj.

ACROSS

1. Muppet who is the drummer for Dr. Teeth and the Electric Mayhem
7. Biblical brother
11. Close friend, in internet slang
14. Roguish character
15. Alluring
16. Last: Abbr.
17. The 18-plus crowd now ___ (start of a limerick)
18. Marathoner's stat
19. John, in Oxford
20. Potato buds
22. ...'cause [36-Acrosses] get ___ (second part of the limerick)
24. ...with this duster and ___ (third part of the limerick)
27. Normand of silent films
29. Noises of disappointment from fans
30. "Crazy Rich Asians" director Jon
31. Turbine part
32. Teamster boss Jimmy
33. "My gal" of song
34. Cameo stone
35. Yahoo! competitor
36. Tchotchke in this puzzle's limerick, which one fast food restaurant in Israel tried to spice up on Valentine's Day
41. "Yo!"
42. "Young Frankenstein" woman
43. Slangy negative
45. Li'l guy of cartoons
48. When local news might start
49. Given to wearing goth makeup and listening to maudlin punk songs
50. Thing dropped in pranks, casually
51. Pittsburgh metal
52. ...we're up to the ___ (fourth part of the limerick)
53. ___ (fifth part of the limerick)
55. Bird whose male hatches the eggs
57. Game with matchsticks
58. Four Corners state
60. ...includes things for ___ (end of the limerick)
64. Posting at JFK or LAX
65. Trick
66. Carl's Jr. competitor
67. Alternative to cable, briefly
68. Prefers, with "for"
69. Squealed (on)

DOWN

1. Big goon
2. Turn down
3. Post-E.R.place

ACROSS

1. "Pygmalion" dramatist
5. Cutting remark
9. Person trying to be something they're not, so to speak
14. Cry of pain
15. Singer Brickell
16. Surplus
17. Start of Peter Sagal's defintion of the neologism "kalsarikannit"
20. In addition
21. Bidet's neighbor, in Bath
22. Occasional panelist on "Wait Wait…Don't Tell Me!" ___ Proops
23. Rascal
26. Part 2 of the definition
28. ___ v. Ferguson (landmark 1896 Supreme Court ruling)
30. Time for you to do "My Way" your way, say
32. Garden with a noted snake
33. Eddie ___ ("The French Connection" figure)
34. It can tell you where to go
36. Tank fluid
39. Part 3 of the definition
43. ___ Paulo, Brazil
44. Pricey bag brand that's one letter different from 25-Down
45. Not fooled by
46. Glasses, slangily
47. Pestering people
50. Deep division
53. Certain Scandinavian
54. Cigar residue
55. Meter reader?
56. ___-Wan Kenobi
58. Wetness on the morning paper, maybe
60. End of the definition
66. "The Plague" novelist
67. Former Ford product, briefly
68. Othello's nemesis
69. Related on the mother's side
70. Nursery school, briefly
71. Vitamin supplement

DOWN

1. Heavy drinker
2. "I can't hear you…"
3. High card, often
4. "I can't hear you…"
5. Caused to go
6. Excitement
7. Biathlete's need
8. Kiss in the barrio
9. Podded veggie
10. It's one part of water, chemically
11. Starts to wake up
12. Flying fish eaters often spotted in crosswords
13. Frayed and tattered
18. Pacific salmon
19. Big cheese
23. Giant blue-and-yellow stores
24. ___ Carta
25. Madrid museum that's one letter different from 44-Across
27. Butcher's implement
29. Like a film that might get an R rating
31. "Hulk" director Lee
32. Title bandit in a Verdi opera
35. Clear (of)
36. "___ Din" (Kipling poem)
37. Chips in?
38. Utter nonense
40. Mike who played Black Doug in "The Hangover"
41. Aftershock
42. Angler's need
46. Skip
48. In a special circle practicing one's swing, say
49. Unique person
50. Turmeric or cayenne
51. Team Coco head
52. 2002 hit for Cam'ron
53. More splendid
57. Visible sign of pregnancy
59. D-Day conflict
61. Play for a fool
62. 50 Cent and Eminem's mentor, for short
63. AirPod spot
64. Way back when
65. Governor DeSantis

98978

7978997

8897889

888

ACROSS

1. "Now it makes sense…"
5. Spice measurement, often
9. Laundromat unit
13. Designer Wang
14. Famed Michelangelo sculpture
15. "Blackfish" beast
16. "Researchers announced a new blood test that could aid in the early detection of ___"
18. "Feel the ___" (2016 campaign slogan)
19. Lament, as a loss
20. "It was reported on Thursday that the FTC was considering a record-breaking fine against social media site ___ for failing to protect user data"
22. Table salt, chemically
24. Like candles or crayons
25. Org. for female fellowship
28. Ad ___
30. "One Piece" manga series protagonist
33. "That feels amazing!"
34. Choir responses
36. Parts to play
38. "A state of emergency was declared near Portland this week as health workers scrambled to contain a ___"
41. Walk cockily
42. Mixes, as cake batter
43. "7 Rings" singer Grande, to fans
44. Introduction to geometry?
46. Greek H
47. Fails to be
48. Cost for a cab
50. Sagittarius or Scorpio, e.g.
52. With 60-Across, "Mariano Rivera became the first player ever to be unanimously voted into the Cooperstown ___"
56. "The Princess and the Frog" princess
59. Slightly open
60. See 52-Across
63. Gyllenhaal of "Brokeback Mountain"
64. Engaged in hostilities
65. Tabloid twosome
66. Fired
67. Tinker (with)
68. Kisses and hugs, at the end of a letter

DOWN

1. In vitro items
2. Lead, as a project
3. Rice-shaped pasta
4. Big boss
5. "The Lion King" lyricist Rice
6. Feud
7. Proverbial backbreaker
8. French mathematician Blaise
9. Argue in favor of, on the Hill
10. Double Stuf cookie brand
11. Prefix that means "height"
12. Like some cellars
14. "I must be dreaming" request
17. Closer's fig.
21. Commuter communities
23. Good earth for gardening
25. Thanksgiving dinner dish
26. Arouses, as an appetite
27. "Cuchi-cuchi" singer
29. Hundred-dollar bill, slangily
31. Great Dane banes
32. Desire greatly, with "for"
34. Window-switching keyboard shortcut
35. Execs, so to speak
37. "SNL" segment
39. Was subjected to something painful
40. Benedict Arnold, notably
45. Nash of Crosby, Stills, Nash, and Young
47. Requiring help
49. Bring joy to
51. Animated image
52. Cabo San Lucas' peninsula
53. "Iliad" warrior
54. Alcoholic Japanese beverage
55. Sporting event held each summer in South Williamsport, for short
57. 29-country alliance
58. Visa alternative, briefly
61. ___ Cruces, New Mexico
62. Brooding music genre

ACROSS

1. French landscape painter Jean
6. Columnist Maureen
10. Jazz genre
13. Kid lit character Bedelia
15. R&B singer Janelle
16. Well-"liked" prez
17. Vehicle defect response
18. Colorful swimmers
19. With 20-Across, after the announcement of new pre-flight hurdles, Jessi Klein asked the "Wait Wait…Don't Tell Me!" panel to predict what changes would be made to make ___
20. See 19-Across
23. Fifth quarters in the NBA, e.g.
24. "Either you do it ___ will!"
25. Partook of the salad bar, say
26. Alonzo Bodden responded that "buyers of the new super-saver economy no-frills tickets will have to ___"
34. Surgery areas, for short
35. Platform for Siri
36. "That was years ___"
37. Gig that likely pays minimum wage
40. Practice recording
42. Country singer Aldean
44. Maui memento
45. Wriggly fish
46. "They're playing ___ song!"
47. Helen Hong quipped that "we'll have ___ who don't care if that sweater was your favorite"
55. Likely takeoff hr.
56. Star pitcher
57. Camping gear retailer
58. Adam Felber said "you are required to submit to 10 to 30 minutes of something called ___"
64. Airport org. tweaked by Klein and the other panelists
65. "Rolling in the Deep" singer
66. Doesn't stop talking
67. Actor McKellen
68. Drunk, so to speak
69. Oregon's "Emerald City"
70. Stuff slung in some campaigns
71. Awkward reply to "Who's there?"
72. Sat, as for pictures

DOWN

1. Convertible covering
2. Mafia code of silence
3. Put new actors in
4. Norwegian royal name
5. Roofer's material
6. Phat, to old-school rappers
7. "___ unrelated note…"
8. Some guitar pedal affects
9. Explorer Hernando
10. Pollster's concern
11. Steinbeck migrant
12. The "P" in RPM
14. Licenses
15. Netflix selection
21. Water bird
22. Like many AARP members, briefly
27. ___-wop (old vocal style)
28. Poetic circle
29. Be ambitious
30. Warble
31. Possesses
32. Freudian topic
33. Panthers coach Rivera
37. Org. for some umps
38. Mark Zuckerberg's Facebook title
39. Acosta of CNN
40. "Vox populi, vox ___"
41. LARP sprite
42. Moonshine container
43. Story line
45. Called the whole thing off
46. Uneasy
48. Enter the pool
49. Layered clouds
50. Aspect
51. Hosp. part
52. Gets out of bed
53. "Signal weak," in CB talk
54. Gave one's autograph
58. Hunter of Genesis
59. ___ O (tic-tac-toe sides)
60. Computer memory units, informally
61. Of grades 1–12, briefly
62. Arrange, as hair
63. Toy block maker
64. Comedian Heidecker

DOWN

1. Keys on a piano?
2. Baseball umpire's ruling about a fly ball
3. Maintains, as an itinerary
4. Help out in a bad way
5. Collaborate (with)
6. End-of-semester challenge
7. ___ Charles (WNBA star)
8. Contest submission
9. Accumulation when one has a cold
10. Submarine chamber
11. Hangar 18 craft, allegedly
12. Architect Maya
14. Gallery opening cheese
20. Snake in the grass, say
21. Victory formation?
25. Gods of ancient Rome
26. Dr. Ruth topic
28. Tree with oval leaves
30. Frost-covered
31. "You Oughta Know" singer
34. Bay Area hrs.
35. Pants zipper
38. Gobbled up
39. MMA match ender, perhaps
40. Baseball slugger's stat
41. Long stretch, geologically speaking
42. Compared with
44. Impose, as a punishment
45. Fit for purchase
47. Agave fibers
48. Cockpit announcement, for short
51. Puts in the hoop from close range, as a basketball
53. Seating expert
55. Crude company with toy trucks
58. Relinquish
59. Spring forecast
60. Smartphone ancestors, briefly
61. Dubya's brother
62. "A Wrinkle in Time" director DuVernay

ACROSS

1. Singer who wrote Jones' "She's a Lady"
5. "Grand" dance movement
9. Longtime Letterman sidekick Shaffer, who answered all the questions in this puzzle wrong (correct answers in the circled squares)
13. Leopold's 1920s co-defendant
14. Trap
15. Old LP player
16. Convenience store chilled drink
17. Mirthful
18. Scientology guru ___ Hubbard
19. Which of these was a real sidekick to comic book hero ___? A) His actual mother, B) Lieutenant Normal, insurance actuary, or C) His uncle, an older guy who told dad jokes
22. "___ Still Rock and Roll to Me" (Billy Joel single)
23. ___ Leppard
24. "Mercy me!"
27. Tried for an Emmy, perhaps
29. Electricity eponym
32. Peter Sagal, e.g.
33. Like socks that you won't have to replace too often
36. General Mills cereal
37. Comic book hero ___, back in the 1940s, had a sidekick named what? A) Pinky the Whiz Kid, B) Scarlet's Pimple, or C) the Surprising Squirt
40. Gun, as an engine
43. Dishes with a soy sauce glaze
46. City on the Oregon Trail
49. The "S" in OS: Abbr.
50. Like several Asian languages
52. Unmoved, as an artifact
54. "Thar ___ blows!"
56. Ft. Myers st.
57. Which of these actually exists ___? A) "Batman and Robin and Ted and Alice," B) "Serial: The Animated Series," where Sarah Koenig solves crimes with a talking radio, C) "Forrest Gump II," in which Gump fights in the Gulf War with an orangutan
61. Web script language
63. Warms (up)
64. "I call it!"
65. Wickedness
66. Tightens, as prose
67. Civil rights gp.
68. Instrument absent in White Stripes songs
69. Philosopher Descartes
70. Unit in a set of instructions

ACROSS

1. Eye too obviously
5. Put underground
9. Load heavily
13. Quick haircut
14. "That makes sense…"
15. At any point
16. "This week, a man in France filed a $45 million lawsuit against Uber alleging that they inadvertently revealed to his wife that he was ____"
19. Made square
20. Took a break from the game
21. Fix again, as a hemline
22. With 49-Across, "A janitor in San Francisco who made $150,000 in overtime last year was called out after it was discovered that he was ____"
28. Polite address for a woman
30. Highbrow and supercilious
31. Hygienist's org.
34. "The Clothed Maja" painter
35. Tesla roller
36. "This week, TSA agents in South Carolina stopped an 80-year-old woman, who did not realize her cane had a ____, from boarding a plane"
41. "The ____ Love" (R.E.M. single)
42. Writer Quindlen
43. Smartphone feature with maps
44. Spicy taco toppings
47. Merry
49. See 22-Across
51. Reacted to an alarm
55. Fighting Tigers' sch.
56. NBA team from NYC
57. "In an attempt to avoid a traffic violation, a man in China ____ to take out the traffic camera while he was stopped at a red light"
62. Fraternity letter
63. Flying prefix
64. "Right ____, right now…"
65. Teeny weeny
66. Amtrak investigator: Abbr.
67. Commedia dell'____

DOWN

1. Category with a blank space, often
2. Very serious
3. Video game chances
4. "Not Afraid" rapper
5. Name for Dallas
6. Dallas's nat.
7. Dog in Nickelodeon cartoons of the '90s
8. Fermenting agent
9. Didn't remove, as from a text
10. Gardner of old films
11. God in hymn names
12. Do something sinful, say
17. Enya genre
18. Minnesota of billiards
22. Remarks
23. "Already knew that"
24. Formal turndown
25. En route
26. "Let ____!" ("Go! Go! Go!")
27. Putin's refusals
29. Mafia head
31. ____ of (lots)
32. Horn blower in a folk song
33. "Rolling in the Deep" singer
37. Frisbee or checker, shapewise
38. Sleep ____ (consider something overnight)
39. Letters in genetics
40. Air base city during the Vietnam War
45. From morning to night
46. Slugger Sammy
48. Country singer Yearwood
50. "The Orchid Thief" author Orlean
52. Brown pigment
53. Brownie's hybrid uniform part
54. First name in makeup
56. Door opener
57. Compact weapon
58. Filming spot, and an anagram of 59-Down
59. Aliens, and an anagram of 58-Down
60. Net-grazing serve
61. Org. that provides W-2 forms

ACROSS

1. Cyrillic initials seen on Sputnik
5. Instrument for Yo-Yo Ma
10. Mexican moola
15. "Hey!," to Jorge
16. "The Little Mermaid" princess
17. Martini garnish
18. One looked up to
19. Like the ancient Olympic Games
21. South Bend, Indiana mayor who answered this puzzle's questions about North Bend, Washington
23. Notre Dame, e.g.
24. Country crooner Crystal
27. "Party of Five" actress Campbell
30. ___-Mex cuisine
31. "Mr. Blue Sky" band, briefly
33. "In 2013, the North Bend Fire Department made the news when they A) attempted to rescue a cat stranded in a tree, but the cat turned out to be a rabid raccoon, and eight firefighters had to get vaccinated, B) a reporter discovered that the station's beloved Dalmatian was just a white greyhound with a skin condition, C) they accidentally pumped jet fuel instead of water onto a training fire, causing a ___"
39. With, in Vichy
40. Kedrova of "Zorba the Greek"
41. Home to the Himalayas
42. "North Bend's true claim to fame is that it was the setting for 'Twin Peaks.' During the filming of the original show back in the late '80s and '90s, one of the producers got an excited call telling him A) the National Apple Growers Association was offering a cool million to switch Agent Cooper's favorite kind of pie, B) Jerry Falwell had announced that the title 'Twin Peaks' was too salacious for today's youth, C) Soviet Premier ___ had to know who the murderer was right away"
47. "A mouse!!!!"
48. JFK alternative
49. So-so poker hand
50. "Me, too" relative
52. Mascot of the Minnesota Twins
57. "North Bend is home to Nintendo's main factory and distribution center, and Nintendo Director Shigeru Miyamoto has been observed there pursuing his ___, A) leaping on mushrooms hoping that one day he'll be launched into the air, B) pulling out a tape measurer and measuring everything he comes across, C) finding kids playing a Nintendo DS, taking it, and immediately beating their high score"
62. Role for Julia Louis-Dreyfus on "Seinfeld"
65. "American Gothic" painter Grant
66. Fate personified, in mythology
67. Class for beginners
68. "Momo" author Michael ___
69. Ancient Mesoamerican
70. "The Orchid Thief" author Orlean
71. One changing locks?

DOWN

1. Pentium products
2. Device that allows file compression and decompression
3. Dishrag, e.g.
4. Diet allegedly based on ancient eating habits
5. Romeo : Montague :: Juliet : ___
6. QED part
7. Dryer trap buildup
8. Prophet in the Book of Mormon
9. "Jackie Look" designer Cassini
10. Halberd relative
11. Melancholy memorial
12. Confession confession
13. Nickname of the Washington Capitals' Alexander Ovechkin
14. Triple ___ (Long Island iced tea ingredient)
20. Hybrid feline
22. Former West German capital
25. Retriever restrainer
26. "Lights" singer Goulding
28. Country house
29. Juul, e.g., casually
30. Pageant topper
32. Big name in Norwegian royalty
33. Hearts or spades, e.g.
34. Cornell and Columbia, for two
35. "Wall Street" character Gordon
36. Cologne complaint
37. Broadway failure
38. Breathalyzer measurement, briefly
43. Annual reference volume
44. "Uncle!"
45. Sinks one's teeth into
46. Foot feature
51. Blazing
53. Acknowledged applause
54. Piano key material
55. Place to call home
56. ___ Cup (golf competition)
58. Japanese sashes
59. Bausch + Lomb lens care product
60. Bad stats for QBs
61. A million times mega-
62. Full of feelings
63. "Haha"
64. Shooter's asset

ACROSS

1. Restful breaks
5. Born on a farm, say
9. That one and that other one
14. Carpet layer's calculation
15. Move like molasses
16. Diner patron
17. Apple spokesperson?
18. Painter Chagall
19. Doctor
20. With 25-Across, panelist Luke Burbank predicted that after 48-Across, there would be …
23. "Alley ___"
24. Half of a black and tan
25. See 20-Across
30. With 41- and 56-Across, Greg Proops predicted that after 48-Across, the UK would sell a product called the …
35. Losing tic-tac-toe line
36. Four-digit code, often
37. Maui greeting
38. P.G. & E. and Con Ed, briefly
41. See 30-Across
43. Sees romantically
44. Pass again, in a race
45. Junior's junior
47. Canton bordering Lake Lucerne
48. Issue voted upon on 6/23/2016
50. Amy Dickinson said the UK was going to sleep with other countries on this fictional app
53. Place for a plug
55. Les Paul hookup
56. See 30-Across
64. Author Calvino
65. Shout in the supermarket checkout lane
66. Gutter site
67. "A ___ people tell me that …"
68. Fen-___ (banned diet aid)
69. Celebratory times
70. Big name in book publishing
71. Kinda okay
72. Breathe hard

DOWN

1. Astronaut's letters
2. Sahara-like
3. Lima's locale
4. Chantey singer
5. Frozen, tricolored treat similar to a Firecracker
6. Engine sound
7. Klein of Vox
8. Longtime record label
9. Promo to drum up interest
10. Grapefruit portion
11. Dr. Octopus' first name
12. Prophet
13. Muff
21. Small dog
22. Certain Christmas employee
25. Bedroom community
26. ___ suppression
27. Boot from the country, say
28. Actress Long
29. Film scorer Morricone
31. She, in Brazil
32. Still sleeping
33. French dear
34. Jewish sectist
39. Cali airport letters
40. Recite in a long list
42. Cartoonist Browne
46. "Ain't happening, and that's final!"
49. Mai ___ (rum drink)
51. Cable channel abbr.
52. Maintenance expense
54. Answers an Evite, say
56. George Orwell's school
57. Defense acronym
58. Gunk
59. "Oh, very funny!"
60. Conventional Father's Day gifts
61. Abrasive soap brand
62. Square
63. Musical symbol indicating silence
64. Type

ACROSS

1. Just manage, with "out"
4. Military V.I.P.
10. Capture
13. "The Wind in the Willows" character
15. Preposterous
16. Hurricane's center
17. "An Irish Coast Guard search-and-rescue helicopter that was dispatched to find a man lost at sea eventually found him ___ at the pub"
19. Little, in Stirling
20. Fine
21. Ivory sources
23. Freighted
24. Sheep bleat
25. Word before tag or mark
28. "Two Florida men were spotted on ___ ..." (continued at 38-Across)
32. Queue annoyance
35. Fruity red wine, briefly
36. Incensed
37. Admit, with "up"
38. (continued from 28-Across) "...while attempting to rob a store that sells ___"
41. Install, as carpeting
42. Sierra ___ (Mexican range)
44. Pool length
45. Prefix with bucks
46. "Poland's foreign minister said his country's bid to join the U.N. Security Council had the support of many countries, including San Escobar, which is not ___"
50. Call at a deli or barbershop
51. Brunch fish, perhaps
52. "Baby ___"
56. December air?
58. Inhabited
60. Gabor of "Green Acres"
62. "The staff of a Jimmy John's sandwich shop in Florida got in trouble this week after being caught using bread ___"
64. Civil action, perhaps?
65. Italian treats

66. Kadett automaker
67. Cease
68. Anther location
69. "The Closer" broadcaster

DOWN

1. One of the convicted Rosenbergs
2. Australian marsupial
3. Like bungalows
4. Speak by hand, in a way
5. Tiny tormentor
6. About 16 pinches: Abbr.
7. Drink sometimes served in a hollowed-out pineapple
8. Yearbook
9. Hot tub shooters
10. Reporter's take
11. Cry on the bridge
12. Drone or worker
14. Reader's ___
18. Repeated, a TV sign-off

22. Online educational academy name
24. Three-nation European union
26. Skin-and-bones type
27. #1 OutKast hit of 2003
29. Robert Diggs, to rap fans
30. Spirit
31. ___ Vegas
32. Wellesley attendee
33. On top of
34. Speaker's aid
38. Bugs might appear on one
39. Had a series of performances
40. Keen, as a pupil
43. Pro ___ (proportional)
45. "Thank you for saving me!"
47. "Veronica's ___"
48. "Fancy schmancy!"
49. Letters on an invite
53. Bring in to one's home, as a pet

54. Mature on a vine
55. Went down, in a way
57. Tattered clothing
58. Balladeer's instrument
59. Words before an ante
60. Fold female
61. Apartment-moving rental
63. Traffic tangle

1	2	3	4		5	6	7	8		9	10	11	12
13					14				15	16			
17					18					19			
20			21						22				
23								24					
		25			26	27	28				29	30	31
32	33	34			35					36			
37				38	39				40		41		
42			43		44				45	46			
47				48				49					
			50					51			52	53	54
		55				56	57	58					
59	60				61					62			
63					64					65			
66					67					68			

ACROSS

1. Corn-eating bird
5. Doctor's orders, casually
9. Slightly open
13. "Present!"
14. Exercising one's Second Amendment rights, in a way
16. Corrida cape color
17. Met highlight
18. Marisa of "Spider-Man: Far From Home"
19. Former Indiana governor Bayh
20. "Known for its gossip pages, the New York Post has also done ___ journalism, as when in 1989 they A) published a fold-it-yourself cardboard knife in case you got mugged, B) printed a full-color rat identification guide so New Yorkers could tell the Norway rat from the common brown rat, C) gave students the answers to an important statewide test by printing them on its front page"
23. Be a rat
24. Amin played by Whitaker
25. With 47-Across, "Your first question about the New York Post is actually about that famous headline: '___.' It ran on the front page in 1983. But it almost didn't run, because A) it offended the delicate sensibility of the paper's owner, Rupert Murdoch, B) fact-checkers at the paper could not be sure if the bar was indeed a topless bar, C) they ran out of capital S's in the compositing room and had to carve a new one to finish the final word"
32. Luxury Japanese beef
35. Try over again
36. State often hotly contested in presidential elections
37. "Here's how I view things," in shorthand
38. Pithy saying
41. "Little Women" woman
42. Amazing accomplishment
44. From here ___ (henceforth)
45. Indian yogurt drink often made with mango
47. See 25-Across
50. Texting teehee
51. Just to be sure
55. "Australian Col Allan, also known as Col Pot, was the ___ of the Post from 2001 to 2016. He was known for his quirky habit of A) sniping at people in the newsroom with a BB gun, B) shouting 'by crikey!' every few seconds, C) urinating into his office wastebasket during meetings"
59. "America's Next Top Model" host Banks
61. Attributable (to)
62. Mideast leader
63. "Oppression and Liberty" author Simone
64. Boeing product
65. "The Biggest Little City in the World"
66. German GM subsidiary until 2017
67. Backtalk
68. Taken in, as a film

DOWN

1. Leather leggings
2. Any episode of "The Office," nowadays
3. African antelope
4. Rolling in dough
5. Green tea type
6. Love god
7. "I can be contacted privately"
8. Soothsayer
9. Puerto Rican area with a famous telescope
10. "By ___!"
11. Wilson of the WNBA
12. "Apollo 13" director Howard
15. Number after a slash, in math
21. Become hazardous to drive on, perhaps
22. Does a bouncer's job
26. Modern flyer
27. Some denim jeans
28. Perfect places
29. Units of resistance
30. Gives up the ghost
31. Baseball legend Berra
32. Modern hotel amenity
33. "You said it!"
34. Animal that will chew almost anything, famously
39. Antique desk feature
40. Highest Mont in the Alps
43. Had a big mouth, and then some
46. Ones pulling strings?
48. Luau dish
49. Watches every episode of "The Office" in one sitting, perhaps
52. "Mental Illness" singer Mann
53. River through Paris
54. Zac of "The Greatest Showman"
55. Historic canal
56. Creatures in "Harry Potter"
57. Anti-piracy org.
58. Rustic retreats
59. Number of questions about the New York Post correctly answered by "The Post" star Bradley Whitford on 11/24/2018
60. "Sure!"

DOWN

1. Free from danger
2. Amphitheater's shape, usually
3. Guitar phrase
4. Laudatory poem
5. Rock with a crystal core
6. USC athlete
7. Mature acorn
8. Biblical cruise ship?
9. Sign after Cancer
10. Adagio or lento, e.g.
11. Love to bits
12. Artist's list of demands
13. Ceases
18. Disgusted word
23. Promote a book, say
24. Link during a media blitz, e.g.
25. Automaker Ferrari
26. Preakness controller
27. Scuzzy
28. The E in QED
29. Behind schedule
30. Pioneering feminist Lucretia
33. The "L" in XXL
35. Tippity-top
36. "I'm stuck here!"
37. "___ the Groove" (Madonna classic)
39. Blue used in printer's proofs
40. Feature of a kite or a kitten
41. Abbr. next to zero, on landlines
46. "Mmmm! Delish!"
48. Speed
49. Become subject to, as a penalty
50. Bill worth 100 clams
51. Vehicles that Mario races
52. Tropical trees
53. One may be stroked
56. Was generous
57. Brainchild
58. British nobleman
60. Crunchy thing in some candy bars
61. Letters before V
62. H&R Block employee: Abbr.
63. Nicky's roommate in "Avenue Q"

ACROSS

1. Former USWNT goalie Hope
5. Classic muscle car
8. Places for sacrifices
14. Rah-rah
15. The ___ of Good Feelings
16. Change again, as a manuscript
17. "___ will be radically different in 2020 when A) it changes its name to WholeBodyBook, B) the number of dead people on it surpasses the living, C) pictures of children under five will be banned because—enough already"
19. Lizard that takes its name from the island where it's found
20. Bugler with a big rack
21. Noun modifier: Abbr.
22. Study, as for an exam
23. "A very special film awaits ___ in 2020. It will be A) the lone screening of "Ambiance" at 720 hours, the longest film ever made, B) "Fast And Furious 12: Lil Rascal Scooter Drift", C) "My Mother, The Car: The Movie."
28. "Tickle me" Muppet
31. San Francisco athlete, casually
32. "The Naked and the Dead" director Walsh
34. "South Pacific" costar Pinza
35. Pacific tuna type
38. "Travelers to London will have reason to celebrate in 2020 when which of these amazing ___? A) Rising Waters, the climate-change-assisted water park, B) the world's first all-corgi petting zoo, C) the BBC Land theme park"
42. Vietnamese holiday
43. Entertainment host Seacrest
44. Said letter by letter, British-style
45. Walking speeds
47. Event that debuts new products
48. 62-Across former governor John
54. "Frozen" sister
55. Practical joke
56. Soul poet ___ Scott-Heron
59. Treats with contempt
62. See 48-Across
64. "For shame!"
65. Certain lap dog, briefly
66. No longer stuck on
67. 1974 hit by Mocedades
68. DVR watchers bypass them
69. Out of juice, as a phone

ACROSS

1. Sandwiches filled with two ingredients, informally
5. Midwest university town
9. Key next to A
14. Circular path
15. Saintly symbol
16. "You won…"
17. Health club class taken on mats
18. Beasts in yokes
19. Studmuffin's asset
20. "To help students suffering from too much stress during finals, the University of Utah now offers a ___"
23. Pop singer Lisa
25. Timber tree
26. Roulette bit
27. "This week, Sweden shocked the world by revealing that Swedish meatballs actually have been ___ the whole time"
30. Hosp. hot spots
32. Halloween mo.
33. Shopper's bag
36. Sniper rifle stand
40. "This week, an alligator blocking a road in South Carolina was removed by a man wearing ___"
44. Moon of Saturn
45. One with elite opinions
46. Check endorsing need
47. Tsetse, for one
49. With 58-Across, "This week, the NHL denied reports that they banned a hockey player from ___"
52. Boot attachment
54. Ancient Egyptian symbol
57. Is sick
58. See 49-Across
62. Pixar film with a robot
63. Apple device for those who don't need to make calls
64. Stew protein
68. Dwindle, as popularity
69. Nanny Poppins
70. Inscribe, in a way
71. Put on clothes
72. Fraternal group
73. London art gallery name

DOWN

1. Toilet paper thickness measure
2. Heckler's heckle
3. Short run?
4. 1980 Oscar winner Sissy
5. Cry from a crow's nest
6. Extra-long skirt
7. Obama appointee Kagan
8. Things heard on a 63-Across
9. The ___ and Melinda Gates Foundation
10. Stomps on the gas
11. Unstructured
12. Requested
13. Seek to confirm, as a theory
21. Result of a sacrifice fly, say, briefly
22. Cuban Revolution name
23. Perennial Emmys also-ran Susan
24. Prefix meaning straight
27. Mario Kart amphibian
28. NASDAQ unit: Abbr.
29. Needs for weeds
31. NFL ball carriers
34. Network that became Spike TV in 2003 and then Heartland in 2013
35. Green movement's concern: Abbr.
37. Student
38. Bad future indicators
39. Chinese statesman ___ Xiaoping
41. Areas where shortstops play
42. Animation frame
43. Kimono sash
48. Bark snappishly
50. Coupe or convertible
51. Fate
52. Last name of a Beatle whose first name is a nickname
53. Kim Kardashian's younger sister
55. Gunky stuff
56. Concerning Francis
58. Not repaid
59. Actor Roger of "Cheers"
60. ___ Peppermint Patty
61. Dreyer's, in the Midwest
65. LaGuardia approx.
66. Play a role
67. "Down ___ hatch!"

ACROSS

1. Just about shut
5. She may neigh
9. Super gymnast Simone
14. Dry, like some Rioja
15. Pupil locale
16. River of Grenoble, France
17. Organic fuel from a bog
18. Bigger than big, to begin
19. Play ground?
20. "This week, a woman in Philadelphia was arrested for stealing a taxi and then ___"
23. Plays a part
24. Soreness
25. Servers work for them
27. "According to a shocking new study released in the U.K., 1 in 8 teenagers in England have never seen a ___"
31. Grand
32. Greek group, for short
34. TV actress Meyers
35. "This week, a four-hour traffic jam in Alabama was caused by a ___"
39. NBC journalist Curry
40. Banned orchard spray
41. Athletically lean
42. With 49-Across, "A wedding party taking a helicopter tour in Bangladesh caused a bit of a stir when they mistakenly landed in a courtyard of a ___"
45. Global peacekeeping acronym
46. Young lady
47. "The Wizard of Oz" author
49. See 42-Across
56. Zagreb resident
57. European peaks
58. Big suit, briefly
60. Unending pain
61. Trendy leafy green
62. Like pittances
63. Tooth in a cheek
64. Some flock members
65. Lowdown

DOWN

1. Certain viper
2. Vehicle for the beach
3. Nutritious berry
4. College mil. group
5. Mindless copiers
6. "Well, ___ you just the cutest puppy in the whole wide world?"
7. Bobby who lost the "Battle of the Sexes" tennis match
8. Jacob's twin
9. Jello ___ (lead singer for the Dead Kennedys)
10. Jerusalem's nation
11. Look like a rake
12. Eagle over the coast
13. Sail the seven ___
21. Deader than D-E-A-D dead
22. Michelangelo statue in St. Peter's Basilica
25. Texted word of gratitude
26. Electron-deficient particle, e.g.
27. Old Motorola flip phone
28. "Aida" premiere city
29. "That right?," in a text
30. Geek icon/blogger/actor Wheaton
31. Comedian Fey
32. Hollywood release
33. Wu-Tang Clan member whose name would score 12 points in Scrabble if his name was a real word
35. Leg
36. St. ___ Girl (German beer)
37. Wise guy in a turban
38. Avocado discard
43. Exotic pet lizard
44. One who died for a cause
45. Drinks very slowly
47. Ordinance
48. Tim Cook's company
49. Pyramid scheme, perhaps
50. "Cogito, ___ sum" (Descartes)
51. "Neat!"
52. ___ five (rest)
53. Certain U.S. Open match
54. Beasts of burden
55. Soft ball brand
59. Co.'s top dog

ACROSS

1. Italian winemaker Carlo
6. Likely to fall over
11. Lea grazer
14. Sitcom in which the lead came out in 1997
15. Belly button that protrudes
16. Fertility lab eggs
17. (First part of a limerick about jeans) "Our new jeans are facing some ___ …"
18. Move stealthily, like a cat
19. T-shirt size: Abbr.
20. Savory Indian pastry
22. (Limerick, part 2) "…the ___ go way up the back …"
24. Dance for which you might rent a tux
27. Opposite of nord
28. With 48-Across, third part of the limerick
34. Pole-exploring admiral
37. Charged towards
38. Confers knighthood on
39. "___ the love of Pete!"
40. Foot part
41. Old infomercial knife
42. React to yeast, say
43. Funnyman Brooks
44. Italy's Villa d' ___
45. Actress Shire of "Rocky"
46. Air problem in a city
48. See 28-Across
50. Clipper's spot
52. "Highly Questionable" network
53. (Limerick, part 4) "…just look like your ___ …"
57. Animal groups
62. Stole material?
63. Locker room emanations
66. (End of the limerick) "…and show a few inches of ___ "
67. Wear and tear
68. Loosen, as shoestrings
69. "All joking ___ …"
70. "___ not my fault!"
71. Lake featured in "The Godfather Part II"
72. Coke confiscators

DOWN

1. Ones calling the shots?
2. Pueblo earthen vessel
3. Close with a bang, as a door
4. Dry, like some Spanish wine
5. Stain from a Uniball, say
6. Soak (up)
7. "Ben-___" (Heston role)
8. Including everything
9. Egg-sized fruit, or a New Zealand bird
10. Sounds from a kennel
11. Picture meant to bring laughs
12. [turn the page 13.] Bunches of used Kleenex, e.g.
21. Museum piece
23. Place to get bangers and mash and a bitter
25. Getting up there
26. Certain Canadian officer
28. Coal haulers
29. Group of female seals
30. Envelope contents
31. "Unlikely!"
32. Lose sleep (over)
33. Wildcats of the Big 12 Conf.
35. Riveter on posters
36. Gloomy, to Shakespeare
41. Comprehend
42. Dodge truck
45. StarKist container
47. Tourmaline, e.g.
49. Beach safety letters
51. Roughly
53. Dismissive sound
54. Strong desire
55. "The Country Girls" author O'Brien
56. Van Halen frontman David Lee or Deadspin writer Dave
58. Evening sky bear
59. Brand of hair removal
60. "Highway to Hell" band
61. Squeezes (out)
64. Flow of agua
65. Witness

DOWN

70. Stare
71. "One person can only ____ much"

DOWN

1. Joint that's jumping
2. Second officer in the sky
3. Dinner time
4. Tic ____ (breath mint)
5. Rumble in the gym
6. Purplish flower
7. Famed Giant Mel
8. Equal ____ for equal work
9. Like some ills or norms
10. Keep from happening, as a crisis
11. Like the 1%
12. Cameo part
13. "Much ____ About Nothing"
18. Skeptical comeback
22. Back from now
24. Quite bright, as colors
26. Jazz standard recorded by Billie Holiday and Frank Sinatra
27. "We weren't involved!"
28. Battleship letters
30. CPR provider, for short
35. Very funny
37. Just beginning to learn
39. Early Jewish Christian
40. One may be taken after a performance
41. Opening meaning "three"
42. Reckless smuggler of sci-fi
43. Former Chicago mayor Rahm
46. Board game that takes its name from Shakespeare
47. Cookout dogs
50. Tram haul
52. Sage, say
53. Painting on plaster
55. Insinuated
56. Sportscaster Jim
60. One may be struck by a model
62. Potter pal Weasley
63. Choke, in a way
64. Lyricist Gershwin
65. Iraq War danger, for short

ACROSS

1. Rapper with a punny drink name
5. Inedible pile of food
9. Bossa nova cousin
14. ____ Scotia
15. Falafel container
16. Shaped like a rugby ball
17. Which of these ____ shoes exist? A) Ski Walkers, which sprout skis in snow, B) Phone Holders, which hold a smartphone so you can enjoy some YouTube, C) No Place Like Homes—click your heels three times and GPS guides you home
19. Hundred, in Italy
20. Wrestling match ender
21. Certain chest protector
22. Ventilator
23. Army green color
25. With 38-Across, shoes ____,

as when A) a drug dealer wearing light-ups was caught by cops in a night chase, B) the combined stress of 13 models' heels punctured a runway, C) a woman got ejected from church because her slingback mules were salacious
29. This 3-Down, in adspeak
31. Pirate's spoils
32. They carry some commuters in Chicago, for short
33. It carries some commuters in France, for short
34. Soda fountain treat
36. South American mountain range
38. See 25-Across
41. Old-time silents star ____ Bara
44. "Assuming that's true…"
45. "Holy Toledo!"

48. Hit head on
49. Fly like a bat out of hell
51. "Imagine this scenario…"
54. "The Barefoot Contessa," who answered this puzzle's questions about footwear
57. Old anesthetic
58. Saw wood, as it were
59. Tax mo.
61. Opposite of WSW
62. Highway or byway
63. One day in 2014, basketball player Manu ____ sneakers did what new thing? A) They adhered to the ball, resulting in a scrum, B) They exploded, C) They shot lasers every time he scored
66. Brand of no-fat cooking oil
67. Newspaper section with a lot of reviews
68. Primary, say: Abbr.
69. "Prince of Tides" actor Nick

ACROSS

1. Scamps
5. With 17-Across, "In order to regain ownership of dozens of Beatles songs, ___ filed a lawsuit against Sony"
9. Young weaned pig
14. Hillside in Glasgow
15. ___ time at all
16. "Live PD" network
17. See 5-Across
19. "On a particularly stormy night, a New York resident called 911 to ask police to make the wind stop blowing so she could get some ___"
20. Place
21. Part of the leg where one might wear guards
22. Sully, as a reputation
23. "Star Trek: Picard" channel
25. Old Icelandic saga
27. Sailing safe from the wind
28. Apropos
30. Swashbuckler Flynn
32. Smile from ear to ear
35. Like one talking back
37. Drawn-out battles
41. With 43-Across, "A British Coast Guard rescue team responding to a report of someone calling for help instead found ___"
43. See 41-Across
45. It's spoken in Cardiff
46. It's spoken in Karachi
48. Like slasher films
49. Prefix with plane or dynamic
51. ___ for tat
53. "You think you're so funny!"
56. Res ___ loquitur
58. Gregorian song
62. Police raid shout
64. Parisian she
66. Alternative fact, essentially
67. "South Dakota police responded to reports of Vaseline left in a clothing store that someone had been using to help them get into a pair of leather ___"
68. "A city council in Canada denied a new fish and chips restaurant a lease saying that the proposed name, ___, was indecent"
70. White-tailed eagles
71. College graduate
72. Dramatist Coward
73. NFL Hall of Fame QB Bart
74. "Florida police were able to identify and arrest an intoxicated man despite the fact that when they asked him for ID, he told them he did not have a ___ at this time"
75. Curiosity org.

DOWN

1. High-tech debut of 1981
2. Shortstop Ernie Banks, familiarly
3. Agreements
4. Deep ___ fishing
5. Safari helmet type
6. "Tomorrow" musical
7. Still going
8. "The Thin Man" actress Myrna
9. Wedding invitation encl.
10. Roughly four feet, in horse racing
11. Roger of "NBC Nightly News"
12. Singer with "19," "21," and "25"
13. Wigwam kin
18. Evite request
22. ___ es Salaam
24. Scottish cap
26. Judge played by Sylvester Stallone
29. MTV countdown show that broke boy bands
31. ___-Wan Kenobi
32. "Before I forget…," in internet shorthand
33. Female that may be shorn
34. Big name in old web portals
36. Seize without right
38. Sense of self
39. Christmas tree, often
40. Swine spot
42. Question a three-year-old asks constantly
44. Call at home, or not at home
47. Reddish measles symptom
50. Salsa or guacamole
52. Like some coffee
53. Wishes (for)
54. "Things Fall ___" (Chinua Achebe novel)
55. It's to dye for
57. Photo-filled book
59. Big name in foil
60. Some running shoes
61. Big name in electric cars
63. Cold War abbr.
65. ___ tick (disease carrier)
68. Local ___ (frequent news headline subject)
69. Place to stop for the night

1	2	3		4	5	6	7		8	9	10	11	12
13				14					15				
16				17					18				
19			20					21					
22							23			24	25	26	
		27		28	29	30		31				
32	33	34		35				36				
37		38				39						
40				41				42				
43				44				45				
46			47			48		49	50	51	
	52			53	54	55			60			
56	57	58		59					60			
61				62					63			
64				65					66			

ACROSS

1. ___ leaves (Garden of Eden coverings)
4. Actor Ian
8. Sonicare rival
13. 24-Down director DuVernay
14. The "A" in BART
15. Any of the Seven Dwarfs, by occupation
16. "Short" thing at a barbecue
17. Duke U. state
18. ___ management course
19. When Peter Sagal asked his panel about the next innovation in denim technology, Roy Blount Jr. said they would be ___. "You switch them on, and the next thing you know you're getting jiggy."
22. Concepts
23. Pathfinder, for one
27. '60s TV feline toon
31. Government officials
32. One ___ time
35. Stateswoman Golda
36. Warehouse transporter
37. Amy Dickinson said "___: elastic waistband in the back, padded fly in the front."
40. Shady place in a garden
41. Chicken's home
42. Home run's path
43. Polio vaccinator
44. Having more pages
46. Jungle queen of '50s TV
48. Certain minced oath
52. And Tom Bodett said "___ from Calvin Klein. You'll only think you're wearing pants."
56. Big name in paper products
59. "Gotcha"
60. Preschool enrollee
61. MeUndies rival
62. Sketch out
63. One of the people who wore a 1-Across
64. Granular board
65. Shoot off, as an email
66. Letter after cee

DOWN

1. Persian tongue
2. Like Brown walls?
3. "The Misfits" star Clark
4. More attractive
5. Black-and-white apex predator
6. Having little 20-Down
7. "I Need to Know" singer ___ Anthony
8. Muscat resident
9. Summons, as the butler
10. With 11-Down, "Life of Pi" director
11. See 10-Down
12. "It's a cold one!"
20. Blubber
21. QB's flub
24. 2014 film about Dr. King
25. Irene who was "the woman" to Sherlock
26. Justin Timberlake's former boy band
28. Word before green or coat
29. ___ de Mayo
30. Illegal fire work?
32. Collect together
33. Certain holy book
34. Take it slow, walking-wise
36. Junkie
38. Card
39. London forecast
44. Scientist's milieu
45. Seek office
47. Bonkers
49. Went out with
50. Evidence in the O.J. Simpson murder trial
51. Lauder of makeup
53. They're kissable
54. Cruise landing spot, often
55. Unkind
56. "Steady as ___ goes…"
57. Video chat need, briefly
58. Last number in a countdown, usually

ACROSS

1. Always telling people what to do, say
6. Target of some email filtering
10. The Alps, e.g.: Abbr.
13. Look quickly
14. Days of ___
15. Cortez's gold
16. "This class has us down ___ ..." (start of a limerick)
17. "We count ___ ..." (second part of the limerick)
18. Criticize, in slang
19. Actor ___ L. Jackson
20. Cell figs.
21. "...of a flock of fit ___" (third part of the limerick)
23. "How right you ___!"
24. Construct quickly
26. Anna's Disney sister
27. Tons and tons
29. Paintings and installations, e.g.
30. Drink for the dairy-sensitive
33. Negative person
35. Serengeti quadruped
37. Map lines: Abbr.
38. Name of the workout program referenced in this puzzle's limerick
41. Typing speed meas.
44. Any "Stayin' Alive" singer
45. Makes simpler
49. Passed by, as time
51. It's not work
53. Like the 1%
54. Gave, as a fond farewell
55. Tasty
57. French café order
58. "If I happen to ___ ..." (fourth part of the limerick)
60. "Charlotte's ___"
61. Specially ordered
63. Traveler's resting spot
64. "that is great for my ___" (fifth part of the limerick)
66. "In this gym class we all get ___" (end of the limerick)
67. X
68. Follow, as rules
69. Religious platforms
70. Notable period of time
71. Santa Maria and Pinta partner
72. Personal ___ (runners' top performances)

DOWN

1. Make the scapegoat for
2. Honolulu's isle
3. Smile snidely
4. Late justice Antonin
5. Nope's opposite
6. Pancake topping
7. Rhyming lines, perhaps
8. Dadaism pioneer Jean
9. Neatnik's bugaboo
10. Early Ford autos
11. Has a taste
12. Brillo alternatives
13. "Cool, dude," to a surfer
16. Soul composer Hayes
20. Eggnog sprinkling
22. Riled (up)
25. Lodged a complaint
28. Altoids container
30. Prepare for a hockey game or a boxing match
31. Boxer who wouldn't go to Vietnam
32. Situation
34. Alternatives to Lyft and Uber
36. Assembled in advance, briefly
39. Pudding head?
40. Place for a ring
41. Squarespace creation
42. Certain administrative worker in a city
43. "Into the Groove" singer
46. Parents' hirees
47. Dolphins' signals
48. One of the Three Stooges
50. What the middle letter in 41-Across stands for
52. Socialite Austin who is married to Ice-T
55. "It's been real!"
56. Does a little housekeeping
59. Piketty's field: Abbr.
60. Small songbird
62. Flooring piece
65. Martial arts sash
66. Key above Caps Lock

ACROSS

1. Swine supper
5. "Waitress" musician Bareilles
9. "Yes We Can" man
14. Hemingway handle
15. One may have tenure, for short
16. "Inception" and "Interstellar" director Christopher
17. They may be brown or blonde
18. Chemistry Nobelist Hahn
19. Send one's materials to a university
20. "___ has been a fixture at Cannes since the '70s, but he hasn't always had the best relationship with the press there. In 1978, he decided to stop doing interviews when A) he ran out of cocaine, saying "no more coke, no more interviews," B) he called the police on a reporter who asked him, "how tall are you, anyway?," C) he snapped and responded to a question by shouting, 'you talking to me? You talking to me?'"
23. Hordes of gnats, e.g.
24. Shoot with an electrical current
25. People who're looked up to
28. Auto-sharing company owned by Avis
32. "Cannes is famous for the film competition but also for elaborate publicity stunts such as A) swarming the ___ on the red carpet with 200 fake zombies, resulting in three actors getting bitten, B) poisoning the food at the party's buffet just to entice partygoers to visit some port-a-potties that were covered with ads, C) storming the famous Hotel du Cap-Eden-Roc with fake terrorists dressed like ISIS members"
36. "Euphoria" network
37. "Famous" cookie name
38. "The Sopranos" group
39. Hit, as with snowballs
40. "This is what I think," briefly
41. "The festival can be dangerous, as when A) over the years, at least 14 women and four men fainted from being crammed into too-tight outfits for the runway, B) the actress Simone Silva took off her top in a photo shoot with costar Robert Mitchum, and two photographers suffered ___ in the ensuing crush, C) the sound of all the cameras going off attracts hordes of wild dogs known as 'les chiens du cinema'"
45. "Life Below Zero" channel, familiarly
47. Apply, as force
48. "Breezeblocks" band
50. Reached a maximum
54. "The Wrath of Khan" actor who answered this puzzle's questions about Cannes Film Festival
58. Prefix meaning thousandth
59. Vaulting need
60. Prefix related to 54-Down
61. Follow as a result
62. Swear to be true
63. "Call Me by Your Name" role for Timothée Chalamet
64. Big piles
65. Daily update contents
66. Unit between floors

DOWN

1. Bombards with unwanted emails, say
2. 1980s-90s courtroom drama
3. "Nixon in China," e.g.
4. Bakery options
5. Podcast advertiser, e.g.
6. Partner of crafts or sciences
7. Org. for campus cadets
8. "The game is ___!"
9. Billionaire who founded Olympic Airways
10. "Toy Story" shepherdess
11. "The Sound of Music" backdrop
12. Alpha ___
13. "Doesn't matter which one…"
21. Website for cinephiles
22. Bring down the house?
26. Long ride, for short
27. Add fuel to, as the fire
29. American figure skater Nathan
30. Up to the challenge
31. Goes bad
32. Son of Adam and Eve
33. Jane Austen classic
34. Pirate's plunder
35. Mountain goat
39. Word on Idaho license plates
41. Tummies
42. Indian bread option
43. Huey, Dewey, and Louie, to Donald
44. La ___ Tar Pits
46. Big name in polling
49. 2020 Olympics host country
51. Prepared to be knighted
52. Start of a counting rhyme
53. Start to wilt
54. Sommelier's selection
55. "As Time Goes By" requester in "Casablanca"
56. "Out of my way!"
57. Like people who might be in your way
58. [shrug]

13. Chick's sound
19. It's just not done
21. Party dish
24. Plow path
25. Philosopher Lao-___
26. "This can't be good…"
27. French silk city
28. Florida's Miami- ___ County
29. Marked by ancient letters
30. The "S" in EST: Abbr.
31. People with power
34. Yield or stop, e.g.
35. "Dies ___" (mass hymn)
36. Stationery store items
38. Lost-but-not-forgotten soldier status, in brief
39. Nat. established in 1948
40. "The Life and Opinions of ___ Shandy, Gentleman"
42. Slop place
43. The Senators, on the scoreboard
44. Big bag
45. Young cow
46. Tibetan beast
47. Regatta racer
48. Fret
50. Totes close pals, for short
51. Red birthstone
52. Coll. near the Rio Grande
53. Blaupunkt rival
55. Staffer on Capitol Hill
56. Horse's restraint
57. Flea market tag words
59. Sound heard during fireworks
60. Lobster ___ diavolo

ACROSS

1. Preliminary races
6. Crawfish sandwich
11. What a Fender might plug in to
14. Frozen domed shelter
15. Last Greek letter
16. Feel sorry about
17. With 18-Across, start of a limerick: "Since you're over the ___…"
18. See 17-Across
20. Former Lakers forward Lamar
21. "The Divine Comedy" author
22. On the double
23. Like desert conditions
25. Starship Enterprise trip
26. (Limerick, part 2) "and you're done with the ___"
32. Marriott rival
33. Quarterly magazine with the slogan "Cure Ignorance"
34. Drink slowly
37. Signals "yes" with one's head
38. (Limerick, part 3) "We are blowing your ___"
40. Classic part of a tree swing
41. Early afternoon hour
42. Spanish "aye-aye"
43. Pipe ___
44. (Limerick, part 4) "With our three ___"
47. Show flexibility
49. Grabs a snack, say
50. Group that votes alike
51. Puzzle cube designer
54. Skater Lipinski
58. With 60-Across, end of the limerick: "We've just made a ___"
60. See 58-Across
61. "___ crying out loud!"

62. Having a high B.M.I., say
63. Pizza slicings, geometrically
64. Person with fake passports, perhaps
65. Full of energy
66. Words of agreement from a congregation

DOWN

1. Cheery greeting
2. "Zoinks!"
3. Dog food brand name
4. Tall spars on sailing ships
5. Source of some non-dairy milk
6. Hipster's hair application
7. Black cat, to some
8. Whup but good
9. Look like a creep?
10. Talk and talk
11. Get off one's butt
12. Call waiting tunes

ACROSS

1. Blender setting for making baby food
6. Pick up, as a perp
9. "At the Cross-Country Skiing World Championships in Finland this week, the Venezuelan entrant ran into trouble when he encountered ___ for the first time"
13. Dance in 3/4 time
14. Be under the weather
15. "Today" cohost Kotb
16. Continue to the next part of the book
17. Soda bottle size
19. With 58- and 70-Across, "After rescuing a man who was stuck in the air vents of a sandwich shop, police in Napa realized he was under the influence when he told them he thought the vent was a ___."
21. British boys' school
22. Cheer at a bullfight
23. Yellowfin tuna, on a menu
25. "Trainspotting" author Irvine
29. With 46-Across, "Kona Brewing Company, maker of Big Wave Ale and Wailua Wheat Ale, is being sued after it was revealed that most of its beer is ___"
33. Monkey's uncle?
34. Letters after L
35. French article
37. E pluribus ___
38. "A cheap, quick-stop restaurant in France was overrun by people this week after it was accidentally awarded ___"
42. Army kid, as it were
43. Needing no Rx
44. "Give ___ rest!"
45. "___ Baba and the Forty Thieves"
46. See 29-Across
51. Clarification on a Chinese menu
54. Ore suffix
55. Newsstand purchase, briefly
56. Office announcement
58. See 19-Across
62. Changes over time
66. Nancy's friend in the funnies
67. Racetrack shape
68. Go "pfft"
69. Woodworking machines
70. See 19-Across
71. Do lunch, say
72. Adjoins

DOWN

1. With 57-Down, dessert order that includes a scoop of ice cream
2. Newly bottled, as wine
3. Monokini designer Gernreich
4. Workplace rights enforcement org.
5. Italian volcano
6. Washington MLBer
7. Chinese artist who helped design Beijing National Stadium
8. Ink stain
9. Shoe job
10. "___ for long…"
11. Pindar poem
12. Fighting chance?
13. 1983 Michael Keaton film about reversed gender roles
18. Moo
20. PC-linking system
24. WWII fighter plane
26. Singer Del Rey
27. Cowboy boot part
28. Clothing line?
30. Send out
31. Abbr. after a company name
32. Fancy NYC district
36. Cutting sound
37. Mitt Romney's home
38. "The Good Dinosaur" dinosaur
39. Hurt badly
40. Its capital is Addis Ababa
41. Waze ways: Abbr.
42. Embargo
47. Cry from a litter
48. "Consider me a maybe…"
49. Kitchen stoves
50. Some frozen waffles
52. Detect with olfaction
53. Pen filling material
57. See 1-Down
59. Acress Fisher of "Wedding Crashers"
60. Chunk of marble
61. Native Rwandan
62. Financial barometer
63. A snake charmed her
64. Actor Kilmer
65. In need of nothing

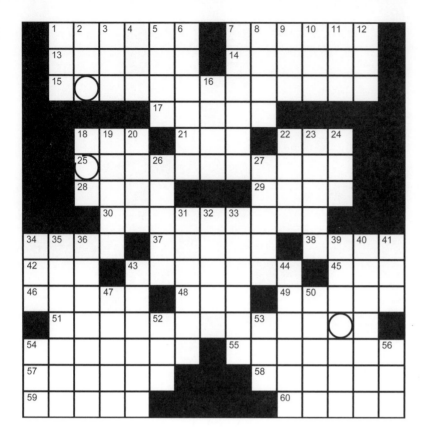

ACROSS

1. Yard privacy ensurers
7. Swank
13. Donald's daughter
14. Cab Calloway's catchphrase
15. ___, movie mogul, was famous for his odd turns of phrase, including, allegedly: A) when told he couldn't make a movie from a book because it was about lesbians, he said, "it's OK, we'll make them Hungarians instead," B) "my own personal theory is that the pyramids were built to store grain," C) "people are not as stupid as the media think they are. Many of them are stupid, but I'm talking about overall"
17. Without much intelligence
18. Ronda Rousey sport, for short
21. Body part to dip in the water
22. Anne has two of them
25. With 30-Across, "Working for a mogul ___, as when A) cosmetics mogul Vidal Sassoon required that his employees avoid bike helmets which might cover their silky, lustrous hair, B) ice cream mogul Ben Cohen used to make employees eat new flavors as fast as possible to test brain freeze, C) in order to test the quality of his wares, bulletproof clothing mogul Miguel Caballero shoots all of his employees in the chest"
28. Trigonometry function
29. Numbered highways: Abbr.
30. See 25-Across
34. Fanged biters of Egypt
37. Noted arrow shooter
38. Screwdriver, for one
42. Question of identity
43. Play telephone, say
45. Regret deeply
46. Run out, as a subscription
48. John of London
49. Provide joy
51. " ___ made his fortune in Australia, then moved to the U.K. in the 1960s, buying the then-struggling tabloid The Sun. He turned its fortunes around by telling its editor A) to focus on football, footballers' girlfriends, and things that look like footballs, B) if you use a word longer than three syllables, you're fired, C) I want a paper with lots of boobs"
54. Easter or Christmas
55. Menswear accessory
57. How butterflies or fish might be caught

58. Swooning phrase after a brave rescue
59. Trimmed (down)
60. County in southeastern England

DOWN

1. Towel embroidery word
2. "Deliver Us from ___" (2003 film with a punny name)
3. Floodgate
4. Black-maned beast
5. ___ out a living (got by)
6. Respectful military gesture
7. Rage
8. Easter flower
9. Put two and two together, say
10. What Singers can help you do
11. Shunning the spotlight, maybe
12. "Round ___ virgin..." ("Silent Night" line)
16. Unappetizing food
18. All the members of the Wu-Tang Clan
19. Certain hotel employees
20. Kournikova with a racket
22. Julius Caesar's accusation
23. Military trial, briefly
24. The "S" in iOS
26. Park seat
27. Weaken over time
31. How one might be found in court
32. English Derby town
33. Remove, as a page
34. Boring device
35. Girl in a 1979 #1 hit by the Knack
36. In right now
39. Sources of wisdom
40. Add more staff than
41. "To Kill a Mockingbird" author
43. Pulled dandelions, e.g.
44. Fly-by-night operation?
47. ___-tingling (eerie)
50. Scottish lakes
52. Laboratory animal
53. Salted part of a margarita
54. Joint near the waist
56. Old curse

ACROSS

1. Like fine cheese or whiskey
5. Gymnastics spring
10. With 71-Across, "Canadian bill to end daylight savings time is on hold because lawmakers say they need ___"
14. Elegantly delectable
15. Totally goofy
16. Not at home
17. "Sign me up!"
18. Shot giver
19. "Avengers: Endgame" actress Russo
20. With 60-Across, "This week, the former head of the Royal Navy revealed that in 2002 the British military ___"
23. "Norwegian Wood" instrument
24. Brown, academically
25. ___ Sketch (drawing toy)
29. Snorers saw them
31. Academic type
33. Major ref. set
36. Palindromic ship deck type
38. With 41- and 44-Across, "after a three-hour search across the town of Dunston, a missing 9-year-old British boy was found ___"
39. 107, in Roman numerals
41. See 38-Across
43. Extinct bird
44. See 38-Across
46. Risk territory that includes Yakutsk
48. Sharp for smart, e.g.: Abbr.
49. NASCAR bettor's spot
51. Norway's capital
53. ___ Gay (1945 bomber)
54. What to do after saying grace
56. "College Football Live" channel
60. See 20-Across
63. Give a darn
66. Where Plato shopped
67. Hairpieces, in slang
68. Royal Norse name
69. Flourish on a letter
70. Gen. Robt. ___
71. See 10-Across
72. Upright
73. New Haven school

DOWN

1. Rap sheet name
2. Prada competitor
3. Right on the money
4. Early stage of grief
5. Yellow ball, in pool
6. Together, musically
7. Fourth sequel
8. Retracts, as a statement
9. Orange debris
10. Mrs. Abraham Lincoln
11. Be under financial obligation
12. Kurosawa film
13. Peeper
21. Tumble
22. City in Utah
26. Advertising awards named for a Muse
27. Not all thumbs
28. About 1% of Earth's atmosphere
30. Hard Dutch cheese
32. Actor Hemsworth
33. Pale yellow color
34. Water brand with three peaks on its logo
35. Type of nightclub that played Chic and the Bee Gees, likely
37. Palmtop, e.g., in brief
40. "My take is…"
42. Like knowledge limited to a small circle
45. McGregor of "Big Fish"
47. Microbrewery products
50. Chuck who broke the sound barrier
52. Taloned predator
55. Be head over heels about
57. Singer Abdul
58. Brexit Party leader Farage
59. "Ugh, now I can't ___ that…"
61. Bouquet receptacle
62. ___ Punk
63. Portable bed
64. USWNT star Krieger
65. Flock father

ACROSS

1. Plum loco
4. Cloning stuff
7. Lose one's hair
13. Boxer with a Presidential Medal of Freedom
14. That woman over there
15. Japanese swordsman
16. Pipe into a house
18. (Start of a limerick) "I want people to think ___…"
19. (Limerick, part 2) "But outdoor work's not ___…"
21. Gets out of bed
22. "Cool, man"
23. Either blank in ___ Leppard or ___ Jam
25. Songwriter Laura
26. The other option
28. Award for Judi Dench: Abbr.
30. Schlep with difficulty
32. "First lady of civil rights" Parks
33. Bucking entertainment shows
35. Dr. who makes beats
38. (Limerick part 3) "I'm too much ___…"
40. (Limerick, part 4) "to ___ my own brush…"
42. Wiggly sea predator
43. College treasurer
45. "How sweet ___!"
46. Involuntary habit
47. Naval bigwig: Abbr.
48. No longer with us
49. Pop singer Vannelli
52. "Macbeth" character
54. Hawaiian Island
56. "Butterfield 8" author John
58. Store that sells the article of clothing in this limerick
62. (End of the limerick) "so I bought some jeans caked with ___"
64. Heads-up statement before asking some questions, nowadays
65. Bid really high on eBay, say
66. Letter-shaped annex
67. Beach volleyball need
68. Take another pill
69. Simile words
70. Jon Snow's show, briefly

DOWN

1. Gold, frankincense, and myrrh bringers
2. Attorney Dershowitz
3. End of the school day
4. Abu ___
5. Justice appointed by Donald Trump
6. Florentine flooder
7. Pin-up's leg
8. Representative Ilhan
9. Clearing off, as restaurant tables
10. Pretentious
11. Disgraced TV host Matt
12. Sassy retort
15. Salad or slaw
17. Sugar substitute?
20. Took too much of
24. Room setups in IKEA stores, e.g.
26. A Great Lake
27. Unmatched
29. Niels the Nobelist
31. Trojans' sch.
34. "Yowza!"
35. Avoiding road crew work, say
36. Downpour stuff
37. Gaelic tongue
39. Where: Latin
41. Christmas decorations
44. Type of palm or pudding
46. Bullfight figure
49. Like a lot
50. "___ no earthly idea…"
51. Unclothed
53. "Toy Story" boy
55. Sanctuaries
57. Boxes at a rock show
59. Tall, flightless bird
60. Cookie sometimes baked into cheesecake crusts
61. Senator Romney
63. 4-Down's nation: Abbr.

ACROSS

1. British sovereign rule in India
4. Do like Lil Nas X
7. With 56-Across, "California residents, upset that a sinkhole in the road had taken so long to get repaired, threw the sinkhole a ___."
12. Crossword bird
13. Lamb's mom
14. Julio's friend
15. With 19-Across, "A weatherman in Mississippi was surprised when a small child interrupted his weather forecast and predicted '___'"
18. 1980s Mets reliever Jesse who pitched in a record 1,252 games
19. See 15-Across
23. Ranch group
27. Nothing
28. Bust in a park or museum
30. Reason-based belief
33. Lei people?
36. "Passengers stuck in a massive traffic jam on a Seattle highway were relieved to see a ___ stuck as well"
38. "Alien" actress Weaver
41. "Great job!"
45. Take too far
46. Before, in a poem
47. Eight-bit unit
48. "This week, jurors in an arson trial in Florida were given a reason not to trust the defense lawyer when he ___ during closing arguments"
55. Laying-down-the-law words
56. See 7-Across
63. "Why should ___?"
64. ___-de-France
65. Tar, for example
66. "After Google would not send Street View cars to map the Faroe Islands, residents there strapped cameras to their ___ and let them wander around"
67. Stark on "Game of Thrones"
68. Lengthy time span

DOWN

1. NBA official
2. Doc's bloc: Abbr.
3. One of twelve peers
4. Start a second crop
5. Up to one's elbows (in)
6. Biden's successor
7. Beef marbling
8. "Editorially," online
9. Brazilian metropolis
10. Three-striped NCO
11. Talking-___ (scoldings)
16. "Give it a shot!"
17. Palme ___ (Cannes honor)
19. Last piece
20. Compete (for)
21. Yale student
22. Twin in the Old Testament
23. 5/7/5 poem
24. Approx. for a landing
25. Launch, as a program
26. ___ Plaines, Illinois
29. Lyme disease carrier
31. Mall unit
32. Tennyson poem that begins "Come into the garden"
33. Sweetie
34. Downed, as dinner
35. Droll
37. Everglades predator
38. Open the floodgates, so to speak
39. Wall creeper
40. Retrieve
42. Opus ___ ("The Da Vinci Code" organization)
43. Bobby of Boston hockey
44. Use your eyes
49. Red Cross mission
50. Bolt on a race track
51. Singer Crystal or Oprah pal King
52. Made a big deal out of
53. Airport-screening org.
54. Hammer into shape
56. Twice, in music
57. German pronoun
58. Soul singer Corinne Bailey ___
59. Sei halved
60. Groovy
61. Also
62. Hither and___

ACROSS

1. Longtime CBS procedural
4. Click's brother on "Car Talk"
9. Clothing stitches
14. Its symbol is an omega
15. Capital on the Red River
16. Sea anemone with tentacles, e.g.
17. With 27-Across, "A group of Virginia teenagers, attempting to break into a car, were surprised to find a ___ inside"
20. Ship part
21. Didn't let go
22. Kitten's cry
23. Streetcar
25. Caustic cleaning substance
26. "What ___ you doing tonight?"
27. See 17-Across
31. Approving gesture
32. Approving vote
33. Normandy battle site of WWII
34. Slippery sushi selection
35. With 47-Across, "Ranchers in Canada were puzzled after they caught a beaver on the ranch ___"
39. Boat's rear
42. Approximately
43. Fed. medical research org.
44. Insta posting
47. See 35-Across
51. It sometimes needs a massage
52. "Sweetums"
53. Swarm (with)
54. Bolt
55. Greek gathering places
59. Pond growth
61. "Traffic in an Australian suburb was blocked this week thanks to a pair of ___ on the road"
64. Totally silly
65. Corporate concern
66. Bird or dog
67. Carpet fasteners
68. Nymph chaser
69. Great time?

DOWN

1. ___ and bull story
2. Oxford shape-maintaining insert
3. Magnificent and gaudy
4. Showtime show about the South Side, with "The"
5. Strip of wood
6. Pay (up)
7. Helix shape
8. Device on which you can download books
9. Small piano
10. A billion years
11. "Gosford Park" director Robert
12. Movie damsel's grateful cry
13. Discharged
18. Croat or Serb
19. Big name in canned Spanish food
24. Work well together
27. ___ job
28. Itinerary abbr.
29. Camera type, briefly
30. "Same here"
36. Like some verbs: Abbr.
37. Gp. advising the president on foreign policy
38. Animal with a beard
39. Deer playmate, in "Home on the Range"
40. One at the theater
41. English's most common word
44. Student driver's accreditation
45. Large lizard
46. Popular cold medicine
47. Noblemen like Macbeth
48. Gun control advocate David
49. Long, thin mushrooms
50. Shed item?
56. Hindu hero
57. Med. school class
58. Like custard
60. "The Thin Man" canine
62. Cartridge contents
63. ___ Lingus

ACROSS

1. Hits with an open hand
6. Diagnostic procedure in a tube, for short
9. Expensive violin, for short
14. Holder in an artist's studio
15. Time between ice ages, say
16. Kind of jacket named after an Indian leader
17. Expensive violin
18. Years, to Yves
19. Occupied, as a restroom
20. With 35-, 45-, and 59-Across, "An airport in England was put on high alert this week after two men ___"
23. The "Y" of BYO
24. Sister's daughter
25. Facebook screed
27. Feel discomfort
28. More willowy
30. Quaint stadium chant
31. Thief, in brief
33. Like fabrics that can have their colors changed: Var.
35. See 20-Across
39. Happy, in old slang
41. ___ grass
42. "Space Adventure Cobra" director Alexandre
45. See 20-Across
51. Cut deeply
52. El Ártico, e.g.
53. Nile slitherer
54. Science fiction author J. G. ___
58. Logical conclusion letters
59. See 20-Across
62. Try, as a case
63. "Barnaby Jones" star Buddy
64. Copier brand acquired by Kyocera
65. "___ silly question, get…"
66. "Ideas Worth Spreading" series
67. Flat, as a line

DOWN

1. Word before chantey or change
2. Kerosene, colloquially
3. By and large
4. Actor Dinklage
5. Buttonhole, e.g.
6. Villain
7. Fourteen-line poem
8. Bee or flea
9. Bad mood
10. Pavarotti, notably
11. Tart pie ingredient
12. Weapons storehouse
13. Expected
21. Final stanza in a poem
22. Acts
23. Himalayan beast
26. First word in many band names
28. "Rugrats" dad
29. Source of some flour
32. Intimidate, with "out"
34. Make ___ (do some business)
36. Tugboat job
37. Low-___ (healthy, casually, in a way)
38. Packed away, as lunch
39. Grinds
40. Language of pitchers and spots
43. Actor Phoenix
44. Actress Bening
45. Mystery writer Christie
46. Singer McEntire
47. Old saw
48. Quiz show scandal figure Charles Van ___
49. "Back in Black" band
50. Stop running, as a battery
55. Pride parade letters
56. Emit coherent light
57. Like wine and cheese, often
60. Victoria's Secret purchase
61. Med. care provider

ACROSS

1. TV selection
8. Legendary Bears coach George
13. Like many older large-screen TVs
14. Printed page count
15. Biblical priest who was Moses's nephew
16. Candy-coated, like some doughnuts and cookies
17. With 23-Across, "A tech company unveiled plans this week to use a ____ to provide security at parking lots and shopping malls"
19. Prince William or Boris Johnson, e.g.
21. Hit single for U2 or Metallica
22. Misanthrope's emotion
23. See 17-Across
25. Before, in verse
26. Collector's pursuits
27. Difficulty
28. Tampa Bay ballplayers
30. Gingivitis spot
31. With 45- and 40-Across, "This week, a California man was arrested for being drunk and disorderly after ____ in a Silicon Valley parking lot"
33. Locks in a barn?
34. Princess Middleton
35. Mischief-maker
38. Maintained
39. B'way theater buys
40. See 31-Across
42. Narcissist's focus
43. Samovar
44. Lucy Lawless role
45. See 31-Across
50. King David's third son
51. Decked out
54. "A ____ as good as a mile"
55. Fragrant garden bloomer
56. What ushers show you to
57. Parodies

DOWN

1. Michael of "SNL"
2. The "good" cholesterol: Abbr.
3. Puerto Rican port (and AEROBIC anagram)
4. Close by
5. "Inglourious Basterds" villain
6. Dutch cheese
7. Orpheus' instrument
8. Stoned, say
9. Object of loathing
10. Cowboy ropes
11. Operatives
12. Bulrush, e.g.
14. Olympic sled
16. Trig ratio
18. Giving up altogether
19. Certain support source
20. Cone's retinal partner
24. Be big on social media
25. Visual artist's asset
26. ____ Tuesday
29. Honest prez
30. Destroy the interior of
31. Flag's position, at times of mourning
32. Levy
33. Comic McCarthy
35. "Please, PLEASE!"
36. Calendar abbr.
37. Educ. group
38. Jazz titan Hancock
39. Edit, as text
41. City that hosts the California Strawberry Festival
42. Pulls a fast one on
43. Roswell sightings
46. New Haven collegians
47. Toppers
48. Place for a kid's fort
49. Farsi-speaking land
52. Psychic's claim, briefly
53. Parc ____ Princes (Paris soccer stadium)

ACROSS

1. Mended precariously, as glasses
6. James B. Comey's former org.
9. Demolish
14. Earthy pigment
15. Heavenly sphere
16. Grocery path
17. With 23-Across, "According to police in Oregon, a local flower shop is under investigation for stocking their shelves with flowers that an employee ___"
19. One on Match.com, say
20. Pull a scam on
21. Author McEwan
22. Tragic king
23. See 17-Across
29. Bridal response, hopefully
30. Device for recording shows for later
31. "This week, a man in South Dakota was fined for walking his ___ without a leash"
34. Wile E. Coyote's favorite company
35. Sing with one's mouth shut
38. Placed on the ground
39. Dinosaur in Super Mario games
41. Express optimism
42. Distant, but within sight
43. Former radio jock Don
44. "After a pregnancy that stretched on for months and was streamed online, April the giraffe finally gave birth, and then promptly kicked her vet in the ___"
46. Complaints
47. Last: Abbr.
48. With 61-Across, "A police department in Oklahoma, attempting to trick drug users into turning themselves in, offered ___"
56. Related
57. Burger holder
58. Early hip-hop collective
59. Rhythmic numbers
61. See 48-Across
64. New Delhi's country
65. "I believe," online
66. Fabled baby deliverer
67. Author's negotiator
68. Football carriers: Abbr.
69. Rock tour info

DOWN

1. Puccini heroine
2. ___ Bell (Anne Brontë's pseudonym)
3. Perform perfunctorily
4. Sushi source
5. Dr. of 58-Across
6. Sudden advance
7. Rodeo bucker
8. Company known as "Big Blue"
9. Collection of bills
10. Classic theater name
11. Lauder of fashion
12. Not hazy or misty
13. 2004 ballot name
18. Bit of baloney
24. Adderall's target
25. Joey of Hundred Acre Wood
26. Cut in glass
27. Imitative one
28. Time before
31. Thickness, as of wood or toilet paper
32. Former NBAer ___ Ming
33. Strawberry, e.g., once, briefly
34. Pitiable fool
35. Khoikhoi pastoralist, in erstwhile colonialist language
36. Bars read by lasers
37. "So what?"
40. Show the door, in a tournament
41. Actress Celeste
43. Apple product platform
45. Sci-fi play that introduced the word "robot"
46. Entered
48. Shire of "Rocky"
49. Giving approval
50. Diacritical mark used in España
51. Big blast
52. Coins in Spain and France
53. Gerund ending
54. Quaint contraction
55. "Big" actor
60. ___ out (stayed on the bench)
61. Balsam, e.g.
62. Onetime aid in psychotherapy
63. Hagen of stage and screen

ACROSS

1. Auntie of musicals
5. Playtex products
9. Disney deer
14. Brush up against
15. Grate greatly
16. Newton who watched an apple fall from a tree
17. Parks in the news in 1955
18. Lead-in for "boy!" or "girl!"
19. Actress Spacek
20. With 37- and 56-Across, "This week, people in Britain voiced their outrage about the country's new five pound note, claiming that it ___"
23. Maze's goal
24. Unite, in a way
25. Junior, to Senior
26. Fix dishonestly
28. Parkinson's disease drug
30. Bump into
32. Opposite of nuts
33. Second sequel's Roman numeral
35. "Jenny from the Block" singer, to fans
36. Talked-about couple
37. See 20-Across
41. Butcher's stuff
42. Command to a dog
43. Huge amount
44. U.K., to the U.S.
45. Resort near Park City
47. Neck parts
51. Spritely D&D character
52. "Local = Fresh" supermarket
53. "Keep that private! Sheesh!," initally
55. Craft in Genesis
56. See 20-Across
60. "I'll take you there," from a motorcyclist
61. Collectible Camaro model
62. Gratis
63. Dancing Astaire
64. Heinie
65. Car coat problem
66. Generous one
67. Bigfoot
68. Makes a decision (to)

DOWN

1. Mime Marceau
2. Be rich (in)
3. Obligatory
4. Airplane travelers often check them: Abbr.
5. Danish astronomer Tycho
6. Like video games with adult themes
7. Piedmont wine city
8. How rural areas are populated
9. Badlands animal
10. Without changes
11. Car company with a trident logo
12. Baby's bed
13. Slick, in a way
21. Creator of Sawyer and Finn
22. Yet to hit stores
27. Stone in a ring
29. Religious seriousness
31. Remove, as a Bluray disc
32. St. Catherine's birthplace
34. "We got the okay!"
37. Loaded and then some
38. Ajar
39. Boisterous fun
40. "America's Drive-In" restaurant
41. Fannie ___ (home loan source)
46. Not marked up
48. Become a couple
49. "Ready Player One" author Cline
50. Clay pigeon targets, informally
52. Word before tube, child, or ear
54. Rice-based ice cream treat
57. All by oneself
58. Not false
59. Dr. J hairstyle
60. Was down with

ACROSS

1. Brains
7. "___ is more"
11. Tuna at a luau
14. "You are not!" rejoinder
15. One who's against
16. One who's against
17. "This week, a Russian media outlet was silenced when a ___ broke into their studio and interrupted the broadcast"
19. Deterioration
20. Org. whose workers might confiscate shampoo and water bottles
21. "___ rang?"
22. Smiling word
24. Go with the flow?
25. "A pizza delivery driver in Delaware got applause and a big tip when he successfully delivered pizza to an ___"
28. Broad lowland
30. Shakespearean prince, informally
31. Birthday numbers
32. Brought back
35. Famous Loch
38. Preposition often used in palindromes
39. With 55-Across, "After a drunk man attempted to break into their apartment twice in one night, a Canadian couple was surprised to find a ___ outside their door the next day"
42. Bikini top
45. Leave the stage, say
46. Peabrain
49. Unaccompanied
51. ___ Mahal
53. Medical researcher's goal
55. See 39-Across
60. ___ Avery, Looney Tunes animator
61. "Star Wars" actor Mark
62. Guitar, in slang
63. ___ and trade
64. Warrior's gp.

65. "This week, a charity shop in the U.K. pleaded with people to please stop donating copies of the book 'The ___'"
69. Under the weather
70. Dutch cheese that comes in wax
71. Inspire love in
72. Skeleton ___
73. Casino city near Tahoe
74. Bemoan

DOWN

1. Got the lumps out
2. 3 Musketeers relative
3. Easygoing
4. Way to go, for short
5. Harding on ice
6. Destroyed Biblical city
7. Place (down)
8. Break off
9. Soup base
10. Tourist stop
11. Expanse of land
12. Indiana basketball player
13. High-pressure
18. Certain Protestant: Abbr.
23. Pitcher's stat
26. Didn't pay drink-by-drink
27. Baldwin who plays Donald
29. People who work for the Times, e.g., briefly
33. Car about-face, casually
34. Porn letters
36. Word with boot, lift, or pole
37. Yard surface that's rolled out
40. Feeling for the unfortunate
41. Fan-___ (amateur writing)
42. Spanish shoe designer Manolo
43. Able to be caught, as horses by a cowboy
44. Oddity
47. Result

48. "Don't ___ me"
50. Whitney who invented the cotton gin
52. Tennis legend Billie ___ King
54. Whiz
56. Not as recent
57. Forest opening
58. Big name in spreadsheets
59. Queen of Spain
66. Small business vehicle
67. Online qualification
68. GoPro device, for short

1	2	3	4		5	6	7	8	9		10	11	12	13
14					15						16			
17					18						19			
20				21						22		23		
		24					25			26				
27	28	29			30	31		32					33	
34				35			36							
37			38		39					40				
41			42	43				44			45			
46						47			48	49				
	50				51			52						
53			54		55	56					57	58	59	
60		61		62						63				
64				65						66				
67				68						69				

ACROSS

1. Window blind piece
5. Japanese folklore creature that's also a Greek letter
10. Outstanding amount
14. Bouillon unit
15. Contents of Pandora's box
16. Beautiful water color
17. Baldwin of "30 Rock"
18. Keep occupied
19. "Watch your head!"
20. Academy Award winner for her costume design in "Black Panther" who answered this puzzle's questions about Garfield
23. "I Like ___"
24. Kabuki alternative
25. Delphi diviner
27. Michael formerly of the Doobie Brothers and Steely Dan
32. Poles for sails
34. Cakes companion
35. "Garfield was invented by Jim Davis in 1978. Davis was inspired by A) his own cat, a beloved tubby tabby named Taft, B) a desire to create 'a good ___ character' that would make him a lot of money, C) his brother, who was fat, lazy, loved lasagna, and occasionally cleaned himself by licking his hands"
37. Spice derived from nutmeg
39. Words that seal the deal
40. Slammer at sea
41. "In 2004, 'Garfield: The Movie' came out. It was panned by critics, of course. But Garfield was voiced by legendary actor ___. Why did ___ agree to play Garfield? Was it, A) the producers agreed to pay him with a lifetime supply of Italian beef sandwiches from his favorite Chicago restaurant, B) he mistakenly thought that the movie's screenwriter, Joel Cohen with an H, was Joel Coen of the Coen brothers, or C) he was still angry that he wasn't allowed to provide a voice for the gopher in 'Caddyshack'?"
45. Ames school, for short
46. Warren Buffett, notably
47. Drain of energy
50. Big shortening name
52. Singer DiFranco
53. Revolutionary with a beret
54. "Not every Garfield strip has been embraced by fans, including A) a 2007 strip in which Odie burns an American flag while screaming 'death to America!,' B) a 1997 strip in which Jon's girlfriend catches him wearing her underwear, C) a series of strips the week of Halloween 1989 written as a ___ in which Garfield faces his greatest fear—existential loneliness"
60. Axes, as trees
62. Senseless
63. Red carpet ride
64. Trendy Brazilian berry
65. Boston airport
66. Vaping device
67. Gumbo green
68. Microphone holder
69. Hamiltons

DOWN

1. Wound reminder
2. "Little" girl of old comics
3. Help out in a bad way
4. Electronic music genre
5. "Dennis the Menace" cartoonist
6. Adidas competitor
7. Santa Monica attraction
8. Clyde Tombaugh discovery of 1930
9. Bad-mouth
10. Annual June honoree
11. Balanced states
12. Agenda for a retiree, perhaps
13. Accept, as a bribe
21. Vast time period
22. Completely captivated
26. Fiddler on the beach
27. Genre for Tito Puente
28. Luggage receipt
29. Go on the attack, officially and totally
30. Bear's digs
31. Beats headphones artist
33. "That reminds me…," for example
36. Zen master's puzzle
38. K through 12, briefly
42. Whiskey fermenter
43. Straightens out, in a way
44. Auditing time, often
48. GOP get-together in Charlotte in 2020
49. Illinois state flower
51. "…then again, I could be wrong"
53. Secretary of Transportation Elaine
55. Sitar piece
56. "Chestnuts roasting ___ open fire…"
57. Laboratory animals
58. "Let's do this!"
59. Workers, metaphorically
61. "Cheap Thrills" singer

ACROSS

1. Swipes at the checkout counter
6. Costa del ___ (Spanish region)
9. Certain spa treatment
13. Cookout locale
14. St. Louis-to-Indianapolis dir.
15. "___ the Good Die Young" (Billy Joel song)
16. "___ in New Zealand is gaining some notoriety..."
19. Recipe unit: Abbr.
20. "The Twilight Zone" host Serling
21. Bridge holding
22. A minor, perhaps
23. Sgt.'s superiors
24. Adorable one
27. Battery part
32. Rebuttal piece in the paper, perhaps
33. Billy Joel's instrument
34. Low from a cow
35. "...this week after he ___ ..."
38. Confident crossword-solver's tool
39. Drawstring tip
40. NPR correspondent Garrels
41. Writing utensils used on touchscreens
43. Express audibly
44. Nuclear physicist ___ Ho Lee
45. Loose fig.
46. Olfactory offense
49. Birthday number
50. Glorifying verse
53. "...in ___ in order to apprehend a suspect"
56. Choice rating
57. Bit of love talk
58. Flip over
59. Totally believes
60. The family
61. Onions used in soup

DOWN

1. Minor fight
2. Sno-___: candy brand
3. At the peak of
4. No-goals score, in soccer
5. Fancy party
6. Tournament ranking
7. Palindromic name linked with the Beatles
8. Exited the premises
9. Third detail, in an alphabetic list
10. Covering
11. Monthly util.
12. Erato's instrument
17. Affectedly modest
18. Barbara of "Get Smart"
22. NBA guard and now coach Jason
24. Master strokes
25. Dark horse's win
26. Little
27. Divider of wedding guests?
28. Informal eateries
29. Still competing
30. "SNL" producer Michaels
31. Last-place finisher
33. Sty occupants
36. Horse's hindquarter
37. Commerce treaty since 1948
42. Microscope parts
43. Handy
45. Personal pride
46. Puncture with a fork, say
47. $1,000, slangily
48. Creative software solution
49. Semi-eternity: Var.
50. Molding with a double curve
51. Easy two points in basketball
52. What means may justify
54. Maui dish
55. Gorilla or gibbon, e.g.

ACROSS

1. Postage necessity
6. Coffeehouse dispensers
10. Chore
14. Documentary filmmaker Morris
15. Use a scythe
16. "___ of Green Gables"
17. "A man running for governor in Mexico claimed that the ___ printed on his billboards and posters is not a mistake despite the fact that it read #[answer to this clue]"
20. Hero of many an espionage story
21. One may be big, bad, bright, or bounced off someone
22. Supermodel Cheryl
23. None in particular
24. Set of races
26. "Drivers in Dubai faced massive delays this week thanks to a traffic jam caused by two ___ in the middle of the road"
32. Hymn-singing group
33. Louvre city
34. Fish that may be served smoked
36. Sonneteer
37. Green herb put on pizza
38. Haywire
39. Take a chair
40. Big hurry
41. What a lighter produces
42. "A Canadian nonprofit is encouraging people who are considering texting nude pictures of themselves to send pictures of ___ instead"
45. Goose Island products
46. School of Buddhism
47. River in Hades
50. Troll kin
52. 1950s nostalgia group ___ Na Na
55. "A Tennessee couple was pulled over on the highway this week after a patrol officer noticed that there was ___ on top of their trunk"

59. Biblical mount
60. I, to Plato
61. Andrews or Dover: Abbr.
62. James in the Grammy, Blues, and Rock and Roll Hall of Fame
63. Word during a mic check
64. Kicks away, as the football

DOWN

1. "In a couple of ___"
2. Drain protector
3. West Point team
4. Hairstylist's challenge
5. Easier to see
6. Pressure
7. TV actress Sofer
8. "I don't think so!"
9. Place for a mud mask
10. Island visited by the HMS Bounty
11. Couple of chips, e.g.

12. Zipper problem
13. Pub inventory
18. Pastoral verse
19. Fitbit count
23. Mixed with
24. Wise goat in "Animal Farm"
25. Zatopek the runner
26. Mountain range
27. Place for a heart valve
28. Sudden bursts of activity
29. Must
30. Just starting out with
31. Bacteria
32. "Elementary" network
35. Hydroxide solution
37. Expressed, as a farewell
38. Country singer Jackson
40. Actress Mirren
41. Makes available, as space on a schedule
43. Hawaiian shaman

44. Edelman who directed "O.J.: Made in America"
47. Lie around
48. Tighten up, in a way
49. Pony's gait
50. Meal for a mare
51. Biting bug
52. John and Yoko's son
53. Clout
54. Cop show alerts: Abbr.
56. Tool set
57. "The Simpsons" bartender
58. The Fighting Tigers: Abbr.

ACROSS

1. Heroin, on the street
5. Bartering result
9. Whizzed (by)
13. Add staff
14. Bobby of the Chicago Eight
15. Brazilian soccer legend
16. Obi-Wan portrayer McGregor
17. Long-legged bird
18. Holder of the Obama cabinet
19. Start of a limerick about a Tennessee high school student's college essay: "I have not had a trip to ___"
21. "…nor been unimpressed by ___" (second part of the limerick)
23. British blue blood
25. Teachers and administrative staff
26. Internet access letters
29. Bygone GM cars
31. Bread served with curry paste
32. Underground growths
34. "…that I write ___" (fourth part of the limerick)
39. Foul stench
40. Intelligence operatives
41. Recording studio effect
42. Restaurant chain that inspired the college essay in this limerick
44. Plumbing piece
45. "The ___ Side"
46. Fish that may be fileted
48. Just fine
49. Prepared, as clams
53. Alto preceder?
55. "…My Yale essay ___ …" (third part of the limerick)
57. "…I love slices. I'll write about ___" (end of the limerick)
60. "___ to differ!"
61. Revises, as writing
63. Overly smooth-talking
65. Actress Rowlands
66. See it the same way
67. What the "-" in :-) represents
68. Uber rating unit
69. Act of derring-do
70. Genesis grandson

DOWN

1. This woman
2. Native New Zealander
3. Kaffiyeh wearer, perhaps
4. One emerging from a bottle
5. "I ___ the light!"
6. Affectionate, so to speak
7. Unlikely to take an interest in anything
8. Baseball stadium flags
9. Caveman?
10. Dire straits
11. Mass-mailing tool
12. Rot
14. Social media button
20. Turns sharply
22. Nutritious berry
24. Acidic, to a chemist
26. No longer carry
27. Snack bar beverage
28. Belt holder
30. Lower leg parts
33. London's ___ Square
35. Moral man?
36. Final Four org.
37. Midwest river
38. Policy nerd
40. Touchy type
43. Traffic tangles
44. Place with cold cuts
47. Fall temporarily, as into sin
49. Gulps
50. Yak's land
51. Kagan of the Supreme Court
52. Duck to avoid
54. Endangered atmospheric layer
56. Hanger material
58. National park of southwest Utah
59. "But wait, there's more!"
62. Cruz on Capitol Hill
64. Word of assent

ACROSS

1. Subsides, as the tide
5. Cause damage to
9. Raised, as a bet
14. Filly's mother
15. Rebekah's hirsute son in the Old Testament
16. Former Indian prime minister Jawaharlal
17. "A recent study found that over 15 million Americans think chocolate milk comes out of ___"
19. With 57-Across, "A woman in Canada who bought a bottle of expensive vitamins demanded a full refund after she discovered that the bottle was filled with ___"
20. Piece of chicken
21. Old TV dial letters
22. Nutcase
24. Pass by, as time
26. Bon ___ (witticism)
27. Manhattan's ___ Drive
30. Talking bird
31. "A Boston man upset about having his 7-Eleven franchise taken away from him responded by opening a store across the street called ___"
34. Diner sign gases
37. "If I Only Had ___" (Tin Man song)
38. "After police caught her trying to steal a flat screen TV from Walmart, a college student in Wyoming explained that she wasn't shoplifting, she was doing ___"
40. Environmental regulation
42. "Same here…"
43. "Residents of an apartment complex in Georgia had to be rescued from the second floor after waking up to discover that the building's owners had removed ___"
45. Improve, hopefully, as an article
49. Garden shop offering that is rolled out

50. Printer purchase
51. "Semper Fi" soldier
53. Greek letter "i"
55. Han Solo's son Kylo
56. Visited a restaurant, with "out"
57. See 19-Across
60. "While fueling up at a gas station, a car thief's stolen vehicle ___"
63. Bounce
64. Thomas ___ Edison
65. Trash or recycling containers
66. Hiking or biking routes
67. Toy dog sounds
68. 500-mile auto race, briefly

DOWN

1. The Democrats' donkey or the Republicans' elephant
2. By the smallest of margins
3. Thick work shoe
4. Repair, as a tear
5. Anne of "Psycho" (1998)
6. ___ yet (so far)
7. Like some milk from the farmers' market
8. Shaggy arctic grazer
9. Ctrl+Z command
10. Bonus of a sort
11. The Eagles, on the scoreboard
12. Before, read either backwards or forwards
13. Firecracker flop
18. Frat letters
23. Canada's capital
25. "Wait Wait…Don't Tell Me!" contestants
26. Tag incorrectly
27. Anti-aircraft fire
28. Modern TV feature, briefly
29. No longer working: Abbr.
31. ___-cone (ice and syrup treat)
32. "To ___ It May Concern"
33. Twice as weird

35. The "E" in Q.E.D.
36. "Hang on, we should rethink this…"
38. Made a row in a garden
39. Letter-shaped curve
40. UFO flyers
41. Comic Margaret
44. From one vantage
46. Call a talk show, say
47. Aim (to)
48. Itsy-bitsy
51. Flattops of the Southwest
52. Black Flag target
53. Irritating skin sensation
54. Feedbag fill
55. Letters on an invite
57. Energy
58. "A Wrinkle in Time" director DuVernay
59. "Take a load off!"
61. MSNBC anchor Velshi
62. Kimono sash

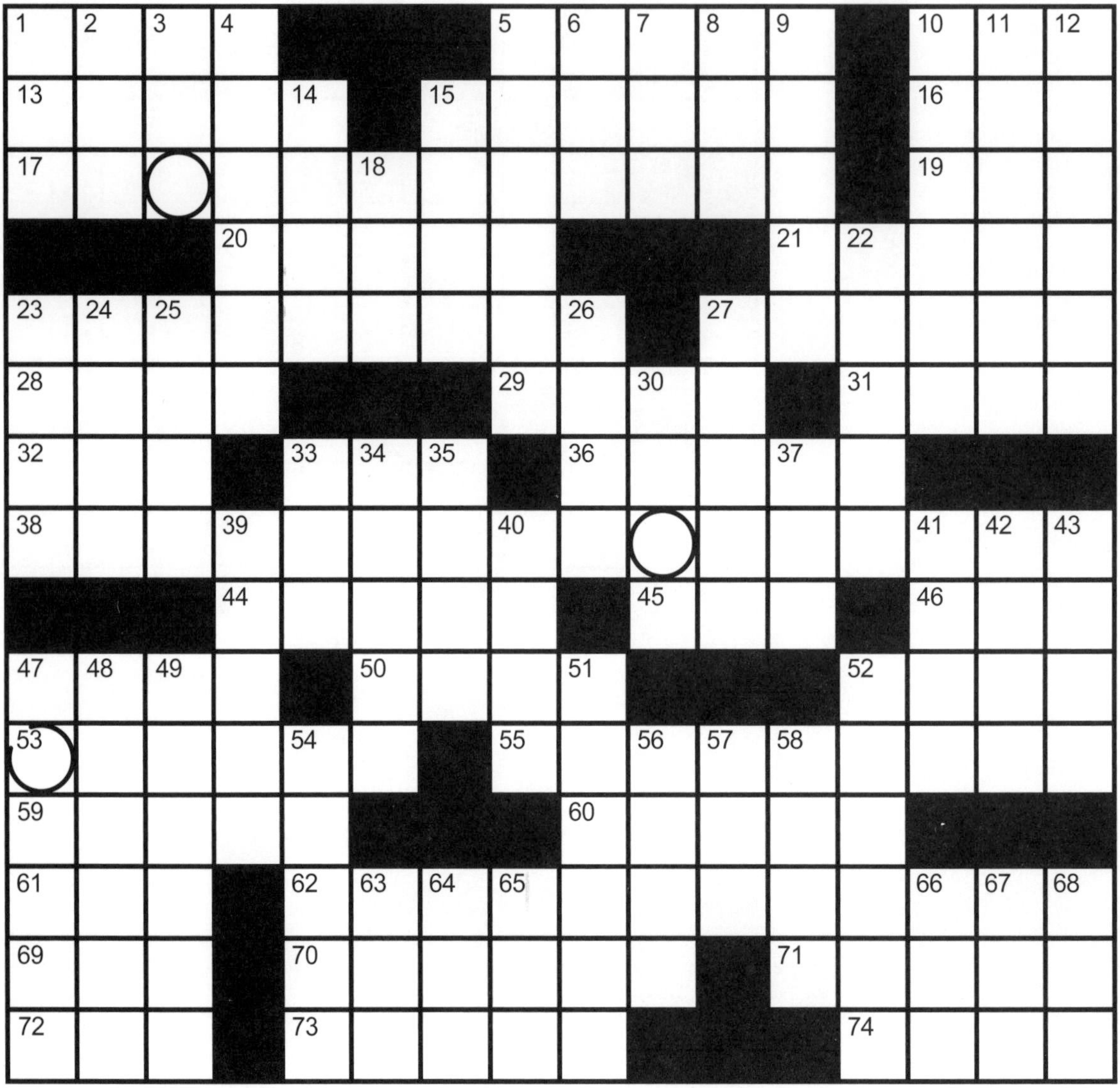

ACROSS

1. Artist Chagall
5. Debussy's "___ de Lune"
10. Three, in Italian
13. "Monty Python's Life of ___"
15. One of Nixon's daughters
16. Unit at the gym, informally
17. With 62-Across, "Which of Chevy Chase's films had ___? A) During the filming of 'Spies Like Us,' U.S. spy satellites spotted one of their prop rockets, and thought it was a real Soviet missile, B) Julian Assange reportedly considered coming out of asylum at the Ecuadorian embassy because the only movie they have there is 'Fletch Lives,' C) Five members of Al-Qaeda tunneled out of a prison in Pakistan using techniques inspired by the gopher in 'Caddyshack'"
19. Saucer in the sky
20. Try to pick up with, as a pickup line
21. Clemens' pen name
23. Chevy Chase's real first name
27. With 53-Across, "Mr. Chase was praised early for being the brightest comic talent in a generation, heralded as the successor to ___. But the subject of the comparison disagreed, saying A) 'I got more laughs from the road sign telling me how far it is to Chevy Chase, Maryland,' B) 'he's so untalented, I'm amazed he can hit the ground when he pretends to fall,' C) 'he couldn't ad-lib a fart after a baked-bean dinner'"
28. Chicago pizzeria chain, informally
29. Soft seating
31. Inventory listing
32. Perceive
33. Small bunch
36. Beck smash single of 1993

38. Chase grew up in a wealthy New York family, then attended ___ where he became well-known for A) affecting a fake Irish accent as O'Chevy O'Chase, B) attending fraternity meetings in drag, C) sticking forks in his orifices
44. "Bonanza" star Greene
45. Stubborn laundry stain source
46. Strike
47. Northwest Italian wine center
50. 46th U.S. st.
52. Anise-based, colorless liqueur of Greece
53. See 27-Across
55. Rock group that Chevy Chase played drums for in their early years
59. ___ or dare
60. Unglazed ceramic jars
61. "___ be my pleasure!"
62. See 17-Across
69. Gp.
70. Half of a Beatles nonsense title
71. Opera hero's vocal range, often
72. Born, in Paris
73. Cirrus fragments
74. Urban vermin

DOWN

1. Kellogg School deg.
2. Something up your sleeve?
3. Narrow inlet
4. People of the bayou
5. Demeter's dad
6. Adjective for Wayne or Nas X
7. Something up your sleeve
8. IX square root
9. Totaled, as a tab
10. School no-show
11. Make pure, as sugar
12. Word derived from a person's name
14. Sniffer
15. Picard's counselor
18. Father's subj.
22. Pirouette

23. Like an easy job, slangily
24. "Hot cross buns, ___ penny, two…"
25. ___ Wade (landmark decision)
26. Lawn sign word
27. Aldean of country music
30. An ellipse has two of them
33. Early Jackson 5 'do
34. 2000s heartthrob Zac
35. Policy wiz
37. Yellowstone critter
39. Digital mailing tool
40. Fam. tree folks
41. Israeli former prime minister Barak
42. Sphinx site
43. British boarding school
47. Word before shooting
48. French philosopher Jean-Paul
49. Walk heavily
51. Opposed
52. Shucked shellfish
54. "Dang! Mind=blown!"
56. Between kindergarten and college, briefly
57. Manning taking a hike
58. Endure
63. "Help me, ___-Wan Kenobi, you're my only hope"
64. "Dr. Jekyll and Mr. Hyde" monogram
65. Place for a kitten to snuggle up
66. ___ roll (streaking)
67. Spoil
68. 1776 and 2001, e.g.: Abbr.

ACROSS

1. "Wait Wait…Don't Tell Me!" host Peter
6. Beethoven's birthplace
10. ___ mater
14. Muscat natives, e.g.
16. With the bow, musically
17. Wander
18. "After getting a tattoo that says 'seven rings' in Japanese, singer Ariana Grande discovered her tattoo actually said ___"
21. ___ Enterprise ("Star Trek" ship)
22. TV show-saving device
23. Shelley elegy dedicated to Keats
24. Worry over
27. Defensive takeaway, for short
28. "The CEO of Amazon, Jeff Bezos, revealed that AMI, the publisher of ___, had attempted to blackmail him"
35. Graduate school examinations, often
36. Old-timey boyfriends
37. Dr. J's league, once
38. Chapeau body part
39. Wheel rim
41. Brief author profiles, briefly
42. Happy Valley school, for short
43. Obligated (to)
44. Famed fabulist
45. "This week, George Clooney and Brad Pitt signed a letter demanding that Oscars for cinematography and editing not be given out during ___"
49. Toothpaste name
50. Chaperones, usually
51. Covered (with)
55. "If I Ruled the World" rapper
56. Biblical beast of burden
59. "This week, the House passed a bill calling for expanded ___ for gun buyers"
63. Caesarean rebuke
64. Unwanted sporting match outcome
65. Language whose alphabet is called Hangul
66. ___ Day (February 29th)
67. Village People hit of 1978
68. Toad features

DOWN

1. Rice liquor similar to sake
2. Latin 101 conjugation part
3. Missing pieces
4. CNN commentator Navarro
5. Retired hockey legend Eric
6. Sweetheart, slangily
7. Round object
8. March Madness hoops org.
9. Québec NHLer, once
10. "Isn't that true about me?"
11. "Livin' La Vida ___"
12. Hawaii's second largest island
13. Iowa State University setting
15. Winning come-out roll in craps
19. Mlle, in Mexico
20. Year-end reward, maybe
24. Info in a folder
25. Country bordering Montenegro and North Macedonia
26. Certain young parent
28. Offensive, in a way
29. Playground rebuttal
30. "Paper Moon" Oscar winner O'Neal
31. Bother persistently
32. Mikhail Gorbachev's first lady
33. Kindle download
34. Abrasive tools
39. In the past
40. "The Fifth Element" director Besson
41. Hive denizens
43. Existence
44. Gallery exhibition
46. Profit-creating price increase
47. Bergman's "Casablanca" role
48. Like spades and clubs
51. Son of Adam and Eve
52. 12/24 or 12/31, e.g.
53. Prefix between septa- and nona-
54. It's not a happy fate
56. Taiwanese computer company
57. Three-handed card game
58. IRS identifiers
60. The Trojans, on scoreboards
61. "Citizenfour" org.
62. Stretch of history

ACROSS

1. Penultimate fairy tale word
5. Biblical land with a queen
10. Where half of a baseball team's games are played
14. Annoyance at the bank
15. Popular disinfectant
16. You, in the Bible
17. Egg holders
18. Maker of Macs
19. Place for a tapestry
20. "To be chosen by God, ___ " (beginning of a limerick)
23. When some ties may be broken, briefly
24. Guitarist Clapton
26. "…yet I preach and raise arms that ___ " (second part of the limerick)
29. Name of the machine in this puzzle's limerick
32. Stately trees
33. His Holiness the ___ Lama
35. Rain cover
36. Org. that once suspended Bill Clinton
37. Not too sweet, as champagne
39. Cape Town's land: Abbr.
40. Soprano Fleming
42. ___ tai (bar drink)
43. Enemy of the Tlaxcala
45. Connecting flight, of a sort
48. "Though I'm not quite a ___ …" (third part of the limerick)
51. "…you'll bow to your ___ " (fourth part of the limerick)
55. Test to focus during?
57. Rhythmic heart contraction
58. One-named New York Cosmos star
59. "I am Germany's first ordained ___ " (end of the limerick)
61. Ireland, romantically
62. Lifeline's spot
63. Former Mexican president Manuel ___ Camacho
64. Calendar info
65. "___ longa, vita brevis"
66. Rockies range
67. Fell, as a tree

DOWN

1. Golfer Ernie
2. Road, in Rome
3. 1992 Pauly Shore flick
4. Demonstrates again
5. Belgrade citizen
6. Aggressive promotion
7. Game news source
8. String necktie
9. Libations with pub food
10. In the most dire circumstances
11. Classic question about representations of truth and beauty
12. Early tech giant with the catchphrase "You've got mail"
13. Actor Brynner of "The King and I"
21. Sports person: Abbr.
22. "___ Haw"
23. "Would ya look at that…"
25. Witch's threat
26. First or park, e.g.
27. Poem of devotion
28. Sixties soul singer Terrell
29. Free of frills
30. Be horizontal
31. "All Eyez on Me" rapper, stylized
34. Con man
37. Dry out, in a way
38. Spanish homes
41. Low self-___
44. Stripped the rind from, as a lemon
46. Noah's landing spot
47. "The Hundred Secret Senses" author
48. "___ Pig" (children's show)
49. Once ___ (annually)
50. Flies off the shelf, so to speak
52. Bar Mitzvah scroll
53. Olympic-level
54. Sign up for another year, say
56. "You're in my way!"
57. Millennium Falcon pilot Han
60. Sank one's teeth into

ACROSS

1. "Little piggies"
5. Shaved (down)
10. Nursery cry
13. Great enthusiasm
15. Garlic-flavored fish topping
16. English cathedral site
17. "A Kansas man who robbed a bank hoping to go to jail because he wanted to get away from his wife has been sentenced to ___"
19. Trip instigator?
20. "Give ___ try…"
21. Total amount
22. Cholesterol drug brand that fights cardiovascular disease
24. "This week, a nude sunbather in Australia was injured when an eagle apparently mistook his naked bits for a pair of ___ and tried to fly away with them"
29. "Sleepless in Seattle" director Ephron
30. Word form before Chinese or European
31. Convey a false impression
32. Gulf land
33. Gloom mate
35. Indian nobleman
37. Otolaryngologist's specialty: Abbr.
38. "When pulled over for drunk driving and asked by police how much she had had to drink, a Florida woman responded '___'"
41. Where to see old MGM movies, now
44. Remove rime from
45. Exactly
48. Frost coating
50. Squeeze (out)
51. Captain Hook's henchman
53. Rubik of Rubik's Cube fame
54. With 63-Across, "Customers at a deli in Pittsburgh were unsure how to interpret a new sign near the register asking people to please refrain from ___"
58. Sixth-century pope who was the first of his line
60. Run the Jewels rapper
61. Tease mercilessly
62. One in Rome
63. See 54-Across
68. ___ Speedwagon
69. Penske rival
70. Like plaid shirts and Dr. Martens, nowadays
71. Fin. statement column on a paycheck
72. Piebald horse
73. Promgoer, usually

DOWN

1. Place where Gauguin painted
2. Full and rich, as a voice
3. Saverin who cofounded Facebook
4. Letters made out in coconuts to be seen by an airplane, perhaps
5. "I speak," in French
6. Inhaled stuff
7. Future salmon
8. The ___ Club (Dubai golf resort)
9. Flake
10. With 43-Down, "A woman in Alabama isn't sure why she received a package from Gillette filled with free razors and a note saying '___…'"
11. No winner he
12. Curbside water source
14. "The ___ Housewives of Atlanta"
18. Samuel Adams drink
23. Experimental musician Yoko
25. Animated character
26. Looks quickly
27. Action figure soldier
28. Hall of Fame linebacker Junior
34. Like some 1960s fashion
35. Japanese healing technique
36. Altitude: Abbr.
39. Prepared to start a golf hole
40. Ranch animal, informally
41. Group of peers that hears your case
42. Royal headgear
43. After 10-Down, "'…to ___' for her 50th birthday"
46. "U guys with me?"
47. Like a 435,600-square-foot plot
49. Florida governor DeSantis
52. Incites to riot, perhaps
55. Half of Gnarls Barkley
56. German birthplace of Einstein
57. Tangle in the ring
59. "Still sleeping?" response
64. Sushi bar tuna
65. Salon offering
66. Lean-to's kin
67. Three-day Vietnamese festival

ACROSS

1. Soft-serve chain
5. Cigarette purchase quantity
9. Reduced by
13. Job-based move, for short
14. From K-12
15. "Dubliners" author James
16. Abbr. after a list of people
17. Castro of Cuba
18. Like helium
19. With 36-Across, when asked by Peter Sagal what billionaire Jeff would acquire after Whole Foods, Alonzo Bodden quipped that "___ ..."
22. Prior to, in poetry
23. "I have a dream" monogram
24. Stunt biker's bike
25. Sound ot feeling wowed
27. Lennon's "Instant ___"
29. Big name in organic frozen food
31. "Crash Bandicoot" maker
32. Stuff in a museum
34. Nickname that's an alphabetic run
35. Basic solutions
36. See 19-Across
40. Leaning Tower locale
41. Eduardo's peeper
42. Brain scan letters
43. Short orders, for short
44. Speculative words
46. Future J.D.s' exams
50. Letters associated with a 35mm camera
51. Fight result, for short
52. Browns' org.
54. TV actress Dennings
55. "...because when he bought Whole Foods, Amazon's algorithm said '___ ...'"
59. Swedish tennis legend Borg
60. Perfectly
61. Dark cloud, say
62. Hasbro game requiring quick reflexes
63. Whip ___ shape
64. Be neighborly?
65. "Porgy and ___"
66. Number two, to a prez
67. Deck swabbing tools

DOWN

1. "Jeopardy!" host Alex
2. Chicago singer Peter
3. Sports jacket
4. Daredevil's initialism
5. Trouble
6. Anchorage's state
7. Guzzle
8. Memory measure
9. Tedious, perhaps
10. Agreeable way to see things
11. Seasonal grumps
12. Filming area
15. Good luck charm's opposite
20. Wise
21. "Yeah, right!"
26. Is afflicted with
28. Mesoamerican pyramid builders
30. Windows predecessor
31. Plods (through)
33. Horse-drawn vehicle
36. "Ode to ___" (Bobbie Gentry #1 single)
37. GIs
38. IndyCar former star who is the fourth to bear his name
39. Kraft Foods dessert brand
40. "American Experience" broadcaster
45. Airing around midnight, say
47. With hands on hips
48. Start, as a hobby
49. Medical inserts
51. Leonardo, Donatello, Michelangelo, and Raphael, collectively and for short
53. Camera lens setting
56. "Trinity" novelist Leon
57. High-quality
58. Planter's topsoil
59. Consumer protection org.

ACROSS

1. Use a Singer, say
4. Put on, as cleats
11. Really strange
14. "Don't reckon so…"
15. Without any lubrication
16. Oolong or gunpowder
17. Paula Poundstone asked, "If I'm doing my own heart valve operation, can I ___?"
20. Bit of computer memory
21. "Paper Planes" rapper
22. Hipper than hip
23. With 31-Across, Negin Farsad asked "Will my parents ever ___?"
28. Emmy-winning Ward
29. ___ mater
31. See 23-Across
36. Help-wanted ad abbr.
37. Calm
38. Tucker Carlson's TV network, for short
40. With 43-, 52-, and 56-Across, Tom Papa asked "Does ___?
42. Radius's body part
43. See 40-Across
44. "Diana" crooner Paul
45. Take a shot
47. Risk territory in Asia
48. Presidential campaign merchandise
50. "The front page of the internet" site
52. See 40-Across
56. See 40-Across
59. Unagi, at a sushi restaurant
60. On June 30, 2018, Peter Sagal asked his panel, "what will we find out is the least-common question ___ gets asked?"
64. Totally unreactive
65. Actor Gibson
66. Hikers pitch them
67. End
68. Samsung Note, e.g., briefly
69. Dyson competitor

DOWN

1. Dis from the Academy Awards
2. "Slow down!"
3. Sharpen, as a knife
4. Tone ___ (rapper)
5. The "A" in HVAC
6. Walk with heavy feet
7. Bovine in advertising
8. Cul-___ (dead-end street)
9. Navy vessel letters
10. Spokane winter setting: Abbr.
11. Eight, in Italy
12. Art ___ (architectural style from the '20s)
13. Roald who wrote "Matilda"
18. Correo ___ (airmail to Spain)
19. Letters used to plug an older article
24. Kazan who directed "On the Waterfront"
25. Amniotic fluid holders
26. Zesty flavor
27. M.'s counterpart, in France
28. Arab VIP
30. Meet the expense of
31. Lawyer Roy and ESPN anchor Linda
32. Biblical hunter
33. "You bet!"
34. Purina alternative
35. Cultural Revolution figure Chou-___
36. Coup d'___
39. Boston NBA player, casually
41. Shipping figures?
43. Stick for stirring bar drinks
45. Potent 1960s Pontiac
46. ___ Lanka
49. Driving path
51. Keats' Muse
53. Politician and pro football player Jack
54. Dispensary offering
55. "Oh, Lady Be Good!" singer Fitzgerald
56. Behavorial trait
57. Combined
58. Certain vote in Congress
61. Detroit-to-Montreal dir.
62. "The Mayor of Simpleton" band
63. "Don't hesitate to ___"

ACROSS

1. Skywalker, e.g.
5. Lummox's exclamation
9. "Aladdin" baddie played by Marwan Kenzari
14. Single-named supermodel
15. A deadly sin
16. Knowing
17. With 65-Across, "In an attempt to rid his parents' place of ants, a man in Maine ___"
19. "Despite having only one letter left unflipped, a contestant on 'Wheel of Fortune' lost when his guess was 'A Street Car ___ Desire'"
20. Farm butter
21. Cobbler's tool
23. Gambling ball game
24. "In order to avoid being hunted, a deer in Germany was caught on video pretending ___"
28. Met productions
30. Basic educ. trio, casually
31. Deface
32. Go after in court
33. Martinique et Guadeloupe
35. Mascara site
37. "I pass," in some card games
42. "This week ___, the unmanned sub named by an internet poll, embarked on its maiden voyage"
45. Provide (with)
46. Cooking fat
47. Exerciser's target
48. Jamie ___ Curtis
50. Excessively
52. Thanksgiving's day of the wk.
53. Horrify
57. "An Arkansas magician who was pulled over on suspicion of DUI was let go after he proved his sobriety by ___"
59. Deception
60. Be indebted to
62. Farm butter
63. "According to reports, since leaving his job at 'Late Night,' David Letterman has been

repeatedly mistaken for a ___"
65. See 17-Across
70. Edmonton hockey player
71. A deadly sin
72. Coastal raptor
73. Nordstrom, for one
74. "Holy Toledo!"
75. Colorful salamander

DOWN

1. Triangular sail
2. Big bird
3. Sourdough with rye and molasses
4. Belly button type
5. Very dated
6. Fully anesthetized
7. "That's just horsefeathers ..."
8. Brood
9. MLK Day mo.
10. Fully conscious
11. Phony
12. Rupp in Kentucky, e.g.
13. Second chances, casually
18. Dutch cheese type
22. Singer Rawls
24. Tight-knit group
25. Wrinkle-resistant synthetic fabric
26. Sedate
27. Delphic shrine
29. Shut (up)
32. Vowel sound in the words "run," "dumb," and "puzzle"
34. Disco ___ (character on "The Simpsons")
36. Loan agcy. for mom-and-pop shops
38. Not working
39. "The Wire" city
40. Former TWA owner Carl
41. Clean out, as code
43. Cry out loud
44. Sick as ___ (violently ill)
49. "Xanadu" band, for short
51. Shrek, for one
53. Hairstyles that get picked out
54. Hair braid
55. Neruda or Picasso
56. Color of honey
57. Actor Ken of "The Hangover" movies
58. Burdened
61. Cry on a roller coaster
64. Hot blood
66. School founded by Thos. Jefferson
67. Old New Yorker cartoonist Hoff
68. Vane dir.
69. Bring home, as pay

ACROSS

1. Wood cutter
4. Speed-of-sound unit
8. Crumbly treat served with tea
13. Samuel's teacher in the Old Testament
14. "Twilight" heroine
15. "Cool, never seen that before!"
16. Potent potable
17. Force back
18. On January 20, 2018, Peter Sagal asked the panel, "after we've had the ___ alarm in Hawaii, what will be the next one that will freak everybody out?"
19. Paula Poundstone suggested "Starbucks will announce that they've ___"
22. Tops out, as a wave
23. Fig. in some identity theft
24. Rollers in mud
28. Zeus's wife
29. Hijacking prevention org., allegedly
31. Agnus ___
32. Be jocular
35. Sense
36. Not strict
37. Alonzo Bodden said "Amazon will frighten the world by opening their new headquarters ___"
41. Metered praise
42. Sales team, briefly
43. Murder mystery writer Grafton
44. Supervillain Luthor
45. Passing stats: Abbr.
46. Had on
50. fivethirtyeight.com fodder
52. Pontiac of the 1960s
54. It's usually better than later
56. With 59-Across, Mo Rocca quipped that "minds will be blown, and panic will ensue, when CNN goes 10 minutes without a ___"
59. See 56-Across
62. Rhinoceros relative
63. A.L. West team, on ESPN tickers
64. Janelle of R&B
65. Horace work
66. Mutt's morsel
67. They may be recited at a slam
68. Car, informally
69. Trashy news site with an affiliated TV channel

DOWN

1. Bing.com function
2. Temptation
3. Barbecue option
4. Has a get-together (with)
5. Maker of Prime Slices
6. Musical symbols
7. C to C# difference, e.g.
8. Cushy piece of furniture
9. Title holder
10. Woodland mouser
11. Words of rejection
12. It certainly sounds like you!
14. Like dry champagne
20. City east of Kobe
21. Commencements
25. Not productive
26. First, second, or reverse
27. Highest number on a die, commonly
30. Baseball family name
33. "Just doing my job…"
34. Mud-sucking machine
35. Certain radio bands
37. Brain product
38. Waiting in line behind no one
39. Resident of Buffalo, e.g.
40. Victorious shout
41. Time-worn
47. Developer's unit
48. Put on the stove again
49. Plasticky and fake
51. The "A" in James A. Garfield
53. Safari sighting
54. Less than cordial
55. Insensitive brute
57. Run tracking apps show them: Abbr.
58. Jogging equipment, maybe
59. Part of a stadium PA system
60. Powder room
61. Dir. from NYC to Boston

ACROSS

1. Head-slapping utterance
4. Link who played the classic guitar song "Rumble"
8. Thing sounded at the end of each Lightning Fill in the Blank round
12. "Achtung Baby" coproducer Brian
13. Colossal
14. Temper
16. With 19-Across, "This week, a man in Tennessee explained to police that the reason he flipped his truck five times was because he ___ "
18. Entertain with a bedtime story, say
19. See 16-Across
21. Served masterfully
22. Down a meal
23. EPA concern
27. Place to pig out?
28. Mustangs' sch.
31. Many a toothpaste or shampoo
33. "Ah, now I get it!"
34. ___ fatale
36. Make up on the fly, onstage
38. With 57- and 69-Across, "A Florida man was arrested for a DUI after he repeatedly attempted to ___ "
42. Book that no one else will ever read, perhaps
43. Having nerves of steel
44. TV ET of the 1980s
45. Stuff that may be flicked
48. "Boyz-n-the-Hood" rappers
49. Genesis transportation
52. Urban ___ (modern legend)
54. Pull (on)
56. "We're doing business" sign
57. See 38-Across
62. Insomniac's drug
65. "This week, 100 people in Alabama participated in a candlelight vigil memorializing a ___ that had been destroyed in a fire"
66. Cheered (up)
67. Major work
68. Fort Collins' st.
69. See 38-Across
70. Car collector's item, briefly?
71. Pair of nuns?

DOWN

1. River mouths
2. Type of play with no intermission
3. Computer user's shortcut
4. Stimulate, as an appetite
5. Act with haste
6. Fit of shaking
7. "___ Can" (Obama campaign slogan)
8. Things one's squad strives to achieve
9. So yesterday
10. Amount after expenses
11. Scotts Miracle-___
14. Minotaur's island
15. Donkey bray syllable
17. "The Beverly Hillbillies" dad
20. "Macbeth" character
24. Shed, as feathers
25. Perennial bellwether state
26. Hunk
28. "Sayonara!"
29. Three-part vaccine given to kids: Abbr.
30. Screen actress Thurman
32. Grub, e.g.
34. Fireside chats pres.
35. Go out, like the tide
37. Go out, like a fire
38. Suave and glib
39. Whitewater ride
40. Cafeteria coffeepot
41. Rarer than rare
42. Fish ladder's spot
46. Place to sell lemonade
47. Center of activity
49. Unit cost word
50. Maker of the Fire & Ice cosmetics line
51. Bell sounds
53. Japanese verse
55. Croc's cousin
56. Scepter topper
58. Casual shirt, casually
59. Pickup spot, if you're a kitten
60. Modern coffee-making convenience
61. "Why ___ Many Incompetent Men Become Leaders?" (2019 book title)
62. Not ill-suited
63. "Sorta good, sorta bad"
64. "Close that window!"

ACROSS

1. 1945 conference site
8. Removes the cover from, as corn
14. Haifa habitant
15. Capital of Zimbabwe
16. 2013 Walter Payton Man of the Year (and former defensive player) who answered this puzzle's questions about offensive content
18. "Tell me the answer!"
19. Groundhog Day nickname
20. Squeeze (out)
21. Mountain Day alternative
23. Suggestion, casually
24. "Wait Wait…Don't Tell Me!" panel, e.g.
28. Register formation
29. Carvey of "Wayne's World"
30. "During the early days of spaceflight, TV stations often broadcast the astronauts live. NASA worried that one of their specific astronauts would swear when the whole world was ___. In order to prevent that, NASA A) told him that for safety's sake he had to wear a gag so he wouldn't "inhale space," B) through a careful PSYOPS campaign, convinced him that the most offensive swear he could possibly say was gadzooks, C) hypnotized him so he would hum any time he wanted to swear"
32. Aperitif made with white wine and cassis
33. Brief moment
34. Close up again
37. Sponsor of the arena that succeeded Boston Garden
38. Post for pilots
39. Come to a conclusion
40. "___ goes to great lengths to keep its listeners safe from offensive content. They even put a decade-long ban on which song because they thought it was offensive? A)

Madonna's 'Like A Virgin,' B) Ice-T's 'Cop Killer,' C) Bobby Pickett's 'The Monster Mash'"
41. Yard sections
43. Not seen every day
44. Pol Paul
45. "At Seventeen" singer Janis ___
46. Emphatic personal admission
48. Slip up
49. In the center of
50. Give a good scrubbing, say
55. "Even professional wrestling is not immune to worrying about giving offense. The World Championship Wrestling organization once had to make a ___, which was to A) make each wrestler say 'I'm just kidding' before trash-talking their opponent, B) instead of heels, call wrestling villains 'sensible flats,' C) have wrestlers stop calling chairs, guitars, and ladders brought into the ring to hit people 'foreign objects' and instead call them 'international objects'"
58. Headgear for pageants
59. At a previous time
60. Shoelace tips
61. Didn't look forward to at all

DOWN

1. Photos, informally
2. Dept. of Labor agency
3. Serving need
4. Indian wedding garment
5. Muscles used by rowers, for short
6. Happy hour order, perhaps
7. Typo
8. Like most Iranian Muslims
9. Berry of "Catwoman"
10. www.npr.org, for one
11. Already in high-definition, as an image
12. Norse creature of the deep
13. "What fools these mortals be" speaker, well before

Shakespeare
17. Material object
22. Light metallic sound
24. Knucklehead
25. Pol Paul
26. "I've enjoyed this experience, but I've gotta go…"
27. Slice of pie, often
29. Expel from practicing law
31. Result of a deal?
32. Golden State Warriors coach Steve
34. In small pieces, as potatoes
35. Cambodia's continent
36. Uris who wrote "Exodus"
38. Cut down, in a way
40. Washing site
41. Baja bash
42. Insect with abdominal pincers
43. Hardly hardworking
46. Pester, as a puppy might
47. Earth tone
51. "___ Land" (2016 musical film)
52. Tennyson heroine
53. "A Death in the Family" author James
54. Many a "Big Bang Theory" character
56. Before, before
57. Monopoly token

ACROSS

1. Not quite right
6. Portable iTunes player
10. "Cool" sum
13. Bridal path?
14. Sport for some big wrestlers
15. Toothpaste abbr.
16. Tweak
17. Kuwaiti leader
18. Pen point
19. "Your first question is about James Earl Jones, ___. In addition to theater and film, he also did what as a hobby? A) masters competition figure skating, B) entered and won James Earl Jones imitation contests, C) traveled cross-country with his CB radio talking to truck drivers in a Darth Vader voice"
22. Chin beard
23. ___ mater (grad's school)
24. Six-footer?
25. Brat's talk
28. French naval port
29. Central theme
31. Pure, in a way
33. "___ legend George Jones lived hard. For example, A) he once shot a man in Reno just to watch him die, and recorded it on VHS just to watch him die again, B) he was known for making coffee by chewing up whole beans and pouring hot water directly into his mouth, C) after his wife took away his car keys for drunk driving, he drove a riding lawnmower 8 miles to buy a bottle of liquor"
37. Meet, as a challenge
38. Opening in a schedule
40. Result of labor?
43. Politically enlightened, in modern lingo
45. Excited utterance
46. Biodiversity sci.
47. "Stranger Things" girl whose name is a number
49. "There is a legendary Australian ___ named Alan Jones. His first major win at a Grand Prix in 1977 was particularly memorable, because A) the race organizers did not have a version of the Australian national anthem to play, so instead a drunk person played 'Happy Birthday' on a trumpet, B) he's the first person to ever win a Grand Prix with a blood alcohol level of .13, C) his car broke down in the final laps, so he finished the race in a borrowed 1974 Gremlin"
54. Noah's vessel
55. Bichromatic cookie
56. One fixing things around the house, casually
58. Voting day, often: Abbr.
59. Break bread
60. Affordable, as a prefix in brand names
61. The "E" of ETA: Abbr.
62. Puts numbers together
63. ___ Bearcat (classic auto)

DOWN

1. Division for some minor league baseball teams
2. Influenced by "Paradise Lost," as a piece of writing
3. "Oh really now?"
4. December forecast
5. Some worsted fabrics
6. "Now it makes sense …"
7. Mountain lion
8. Leave off
9. Explorer whose enemy is Swiper
10. Earth's middle layer
11. "Like shooting fish in a barrel" and "more fun than a barrel of monkeys," e.g.
12. Maze-solving creature
20. Does something, chemically
21. Certain display of affection
22. Slapstick bit
26. Hedgehog's cousin
27. Inform
28. Air conditioner meas.
30. Snapping reptile
32. One who vapes, e.g.
34. Bethesda-based medical research org.
35. Classic term of endearment
36. Not garbled
39. Pickup truck unit
40. Give a tongue-lashing to
41. Wax-winged flier of myth
42. Arugula, to Brits
44. Drops, as a syllable
48. Kick out of a house
50. Musical finale
51. Bone-dry
52. Tear apart
53. Female bunnies
57. New Yorker cartoonist Chast

ACROSS

1. Maroon 5 singer Levine
5. Beginners
10. Owned at one time
13. Program with steps, often
15. Valentine symbol
16. Altar sentence
17. "This week, the New York Times issued a correction after running a story that replaced a reference to millennials with a reference to ___"
19. "Baby ___ Back" (1992 Sir Mix-a-Lot hit)
20. Cream guitarist Clapton
21. Prefix meaning "straight"
23. "This week, a California state senator nicknamed Huggy Bear was reprimanded by a committee for ___"
28. Radar screen appearance
30. Mount Rushmore prez
31. Pizzeria products
32. Frees from
35. Tighten up, as a picture
38. Prof's helpers
39. Bill broken at an arcade, perhaps
40. With 61-Across, "This week, the Big Cheese festival in England apologized to attendees for ___"
42. Worker who gets busy around Apr. 15
43. Teachers' gp.
44. Scottish hillside
45. Walk down the runway, in a way
47. Walking stick
49. Bad citation after leaving the bar
51. Yanks' crosstown counterparts
52. "After robbing a bank in Canada, suspects were caught by police just 30 minutes later when they used their getaway car to ___"
57. Lower Broadway area
58. Not right in the head
59. Gaffe-prone Biden

61. See 40-Across
67. Leave with jaws dropped
68. Madison, N.J., campus, briefly
69. Heart, for one
70. Dr. with a dream, initially
71. City in the Ruhr Valley
72. Gavel-banging shout

DOWN

1. "___ gratia artis" (MGM motto)
2. Man cave, by another name
3. ___ moment (instant of realization)
4. Second chances in school
5. Intelligence org. whose headquarters are in Langley, Virginia
6. USN petty officer, briefly
7. Genre for Kanye
8. Lowest deck of a ship
9. Cordwood measure (and an anagram for RESET)
10. Like a falsetto voice
11. Bard's fuss
12. Pac-Man munchie
14. The Titanic's bane
18. Sow, e.g.
22. Crowning point
23. Classic kids' game involving "it"
24. Employer of Lester Holt
25. "Ginger Spice" Halliwell
26. Seize immediately, as an opportunity
27. Argumentative college papers
28. Denver footballer
29. Kind of equation
33. Heavenly body
34. Kitten's coat
36. Switch positions?
37. Jordan Spieth's org.

41. Possible reply to "Que pasa?"
46. People who might be trying to quit
48. Help-wanted abbr.
50. "You'll enjoy this!"
53. ___ Island
54. Petits ___ (small cakes)
55. Fan ___ (reader-created stories set in an existing literary universe)
56. Eight, in Espana
59. Traffic clog
60. Screech source
62. QB's targets: Abbr.
63. Be behind, payment-wise
64. One can be quite big in Hollywood
65. Pizzeria owner in "Do the Right Thing"
66. Apt spot for this clue and answer

ACROSS

1. Portend
5. See 33-Down
10. Palookas
14. Tracy Marrow's rap stage name
15. "___ the news today, oh boy": Beatles lyric
16. Jay in the Television Hall of Fame
17. "What is ___ other claim to fame? A) As a talent agent, he discovered Simon and Garfunkel, B) He set and still holds the world record for number of cigarettes smoked at once, C) He happens to be a champion Morris dancer"
19. Consequently
20. Formula ___ auto racing
21. Complexion concern
22. Pest control name in a red diamond logo
23. Hybrid, e.g.
24. Evergreen State sch. with a campus in Spokane
25. With 50-Across, "___ don't get a lot of attention because they're free, and they taste like sweetened cardboard. But one changed lives when A) a desperate message inside led to the freeing of 50 imprisoned factory workers, B) a typo introduced the phrase "on fleek" to the language, C) a message correctly predicted Powerball numbers leading to 110 people winning $100,000"
27. Take ___ view of (frown on)
29. Slope
31. Each
32. One of the singing Jacksons
35. Do a host's job
37. "We all know that some ___ cookies are really bad for you. Some are really, really bad for you. Among the worst is A) Crisco Crunchies, B) Birthday Frosting-Filled Chewy Chips Ahoy, C) Keebler Chocolate Cocoa Mega Bombs"
40. ___ someone's heartstrings
41. Matched by twos
44. Cry loudly
47. Head-to-toe Islamic garment
49. City on Norton Sound
50. See 25-Across
52. "I've been meaning to bring something up ..."
55. Abu Dhabi setting: Abbr.
56. By the side of
57. Something to smoke
58. Drink with a straw, say
59. Hispanophone people, with "La"
60. "Empire" director who created the character, Cookie Lyon, that inspired this puzzle's "Not My Job" quiz
63. The "E" of G.E.: Abbr.
64. Mikhail Prokhorov, of the Nets
65. Alberta native
66. Turkey meat option
67. World's longest wooden roller coaster, with "The"
68. Beef letters

DOWN

1. Like some lenses for readers
2. Anthem played before many curling matches
3. Bad marks
4. WWII combat zone
5. Othello pieces
6. Planet past Saturn
7. Distracted Boyfriend, e.g.
8. ___ Zedong
9. NFL accumulations: Abbr.
10. Wide awake
11. Become more cheerful
12. Thing under a car's hood, usually
13. Closer to now
18. Labor org. with a Detroit HQ
22. Big name in taco shells
25. Gambling house game
26. Slightly ahead in points
28. 1970s glam band ___ the Hoople
30. Rainbow flag letters
33. With 5-Across, schoolyard insult
34. Plead, as a case
36. Pizza crust option
38. Eavesdropping pair
39. Suit part
42. Sent via Outlook, say
43. Like some fishing or diving
44. Panic-stricken
45. Expression of delight
46. Heavy drinker
48. Parenthetical remarks
51. Natural flair
53. Unconnected
54. Nikkei Exchange currency
57. Clinton transportation secretary Federico
60. Soft tennis shot
61. Lamb ma'am
62. Critical hosp. ward

ACROSS

1. Geologist's hot stuff
6. ___ Romeo (sports car)
10. St. Louis's Gateway ___
14. Apply to
15. Hair-removal brand
16. Followers of tra
17. "After calling police and asking for assistance, a farmer in Scotland who spotted a tiger prowling his property realized it was a ___"
20. ___ Lee (cake company)
21. Errand runner
22. Not tight
23. Set (down)
25. Cuts back, as bushes
26. "This week, a group of doctors reported seeing an uptick in nose jobs from people hoping to make ___ look better"
32. Pot ___
33. Willy follower
34. Impact sound, in the comics
37. 61-Across' sister in "Frozen"
38. "Frozen," e.g.
39. Join (with)
40. Map-reading aid
41. Represent as similar (to)
42. Cynical expression
43. "A man in California was charged with a DUI after police caught him ___ on a Los Angeles freeway"
45. ___ corpus
48. Synagogue attendee
49. Had leftovers, say
50. Killer in the ocean
53. Train for a match, in a way
57. "After passing a large sign that said 'Police ahead. Stay off your phone,' on Tuesday 89 people along the same stretch of Vancouver highway were ticketed for ___"
60. "99 Luftballoons" singer
61. 37-Across's sister in "Frozen"
62. Vessel in an angiogram
63. Puts out, as a baserunner
64. Say ___ (deny)
65. Discourage

DOWN

1. Gift shop purchases that hold coffee
2. Thai's home
3. Paraphernalia
4. Louvre masterpiece
5. Industrious insect
6. Prefix that is 5-Down plus one letter
7. Glorify
8. Flute's cousin
9. Bark sound
10. "Eyeless in Gaza" author Huxley
11. Point the finger at
12. Right around the corner
13. "Shaft" singer Isaac
18. Expresses orally
19. The king, in Spain
24. Gallery display
25. Collection of leaves
26. Spock's voyage
27. Flaw in an argument
28. "Duck soup!"
29. Mushroom eaten with udon
30. Spice up
31. Affair
34. Ship slip
35. Lines of admiration
36. Pink Floyd "Wish You ___ Here"
38. Frequencies between highs and lows
39. Winter footwear used on hikes
41. Sixth-century Chinese dynasty
42. The Flaming Lips' "___ Don't Use Jelly"
43. Queens, in Spain
44. Slightly open
45. Frequented spot
46. Bewildered
47. Life form
50. "You've got to be kidding me!"
51. Payment to a landlord
52. "Gotta bounce…"
54. After-dinner wine
55. Poker chip, sometimes
56. Butt
58. Souvenir from the beach
59. Goalie's protection

DOWN

1. Weakling
2. Film developer's coating
3. Crunchy piece on a salad
4. "The" vowel sound
5. ___ in full
6. Hair holder
7. Islamic family chief
8. Penny value
9. Pic blowup: Abbr.
10. Icelandic poet ___ Sturluson
11. Captain of industry
12. "Sheesh, I was just ___ a question"
15. "Ya think?"
20. Sense of self
21. Precious stone
25. Lacking width and depth, geometrically, for short
26. Upstate NY engineering sch.
28. Silver State lake
30. Hunter in the heavens
31. Olive ___ (Popeye's goil)
34. Tidal retreat
37. Examine lustily
38. You, in Montreal
39. Amer. currency unit
40. Not spelled out
41. Propose, as a candidate
42. Some light bulbs, by brand
46. Generational disparity
47. Airport serving Tokyo
48. Georgia pol Stacey
49. Org. for the Thunder and the Rockets
51. Unseemly fuss
55. Tributary of the Missouri
57. Pulitzer-winning playwright Zoe
59. Regarding, in legal memos
60. Lake Michigan borderer: Abbr.
61. Gymnast Korbut
62. Chew like a beaver
64. Washington MLBer, casually

ACROSS

1. Fly catchers
5. "The McLaughlin Group" channel
8. Jai alai basket
13. Computer that comes with a Mighty Mouse
14. Cry at a fireworks show
15. "Thousands of people in Florida went without Internet access for hours when a man stole a utilities repair truck to drive to a ___"
16. A great deal (of)
17. Intense anger
18. Open, as certain levels or characters in a video game
19. With 36-Across, "This week, a Minnesota teen failed her driving exam when she ___"
22. Palais resident
23. Little setback
24. Just get by, with "out"
25. "Straight ___ the rocks?"
26. Poke fun at
27. Giant hero Mel
29. "This week, a group of European tourists in Peru were disciplined after they were caught ___ the ancient ruins of Machu Picchu"
32. Polynesian finger food
33. Consumed some 32-Across, say
35. "Catcher in the ___"
36. See 19-Across
43. Slimy substance
44. Beantown music org.
45. "The Simpsons" bar owner
46. "Scientists revealed that a tiny skeleton found in Chile was human and not ___"
50. Forensic ID clincher
52. 10 Downing St. residents
53. Phillies manager Kapler
54. Jeer
56. "Lobster Telephone" sculptor Salvador
58. It's human to do this
59. With 67-Across, "Forty minutes after announcing that he'd discovered a strange new planet, a scientist in Cape Town announced, my bad, ___"
63. Designer Versace
65. The "A" in SNAFU
66. "___ relate..." ("Tell me about it")
67. See 59-Across
68. Comic's bit
69. Congresswoman Lowey
70. Cut partner
71. Notable historical segment
72. Stay mad

ACROSS

1. "___ away!" ("Let's do this!")
6. Elon Musk's car company
11. "___ Town Road" (2019 country rap hit)
14. Spanish parting word
15. Out for a crime?
16. Prefix with classical
17. Peter Sagal once told the story of a Florida man who faced charges for shooting a BB gun at …
20. French bean?
21. Trident-shaped Greek letters
22. Retains
23. Actress Thurman of multiple Tarantino films
25. Use a wrench on, say
26. …because it …
35. Ken Lay's company
36. Perfume containers
37. Golfer's supporter
38. Bright light gas
39. "It's a Wonderful Life" director
40. ___ Capital (company cofounded by Mitt Romney)
41. Brexit MEP Widdecombe
42. ___ Brothers ("Sucker" singers)
43. Takes in, as a salary
44. …and to make matters worse, it … (continued at 59-Across)
47. 11-Across rapper Lil ___ X
48. Costa del ___
49. Type of mustard
52. Turkey or pigeon
55. Wad of tobacco
59. (Continuaton of 44-Across, and the conclusion of Sagal's story)
62. Capital of Virginia?
63. Apostle's question during the Last Supper
64. Calculus pioneer Leonhard
65. Candidate Klobuchar
66. Center of Disney
67. Dwelling

DOWN

1. Thai dough
2. Jon's dog in the comics
3. Fine spray
4. Study, as a subject the night before an exam
5. Dir. that's almost straight down
6. Price holders
7. K-12, in education lingo
8. They're all in the fam
9. Wall St. action
10. *mwah* action
11. A single time
12. ___ of faith
13. Minor points?
18. Screen with an Apple Pencil
19. Easy on the eyes
24. "It's Raining ___" (Weather Girls hit)
25. Sportswear brand
26. Prison-related
27. Balanced bridge bid
28. College town outside of Bangor
29. Socialite who was married to Donald
30. Bite playfully, as a puppy might
31. Grating
32. Maker of the 2600 and 5200 gaming consoles
33. Touch up, as tattoos
34. Like hard-to-read books
39. Some food fish
40. Red Sox or White Sox, e.g.
42. Wish granter on a '60s sitcom
43. My Chemical Romance genre
45. Comprehend
46. Castaway's spot, maybe
49. One with a massive dressing room and absurdly long rider, say
50. Thing in a shopping cart
51. Baby kangaroo
52. Bank account guarantor, for short
53. Eight, in Italy
54. Tiny bit
56. Ring around the head
57. Served right past
58. Used to be
60. It can get you into someone's head, for short
61. Green thing that might keep a princess awake

1	2	3	4	5		6	7	8		9	10	11	12	13	14
15						16				17					
18						19				20					
21					22				23						
24					25				26						
				27			28					29	30	31	
32	33	34	35			36					37				
38					39			40	41						
42					43			44							
45				46	47			48							
			49				50				51	52	53	54	
	55	56				57			58						
59						60			61						
62						63			64						
65						66			67						

ACROSS

1. Nation on the Gulf of Guinea
6. Health supplements store
9. First name of the author of "A Series of Unfortunate Events," whose last name led to the Not My Job quiz in this puzzle
15. Guanaco kin
16. [Gasp!]
17. Make possible
18. ___ times
19. War referred to as the "Big One"
20. Futile
21. "Some people don't want to deal with ___ at all, for example A) a guy who handcuffed his suitcase to his arm and refused to unlock it unless he could place the bag in the cargo hold himself, B) a man in China who wore 60 shirts and nine pairs of jeans to the airport to avoid having to check a bag, C) the guy who bought three extra first-class seats just for his luggage"
24. Kind of butter used as moisturizer
25. Find a job for
26. Cy Young Award winner Hershiser
27. ___ to be tied (angry)
28. Where a sloth hangs out
29. One might be picked up at the beach or sprayed on at a salon
32. Miller Lite alternative
36. "Every little ___ helps…"
37. State that claims eight U.S. presidents
38. "In 2013, an anonymous baggage handler revealed a deeply held ___. Namely, A) every Friday night, the handlers stage a fashion show with the best gowns they've stolen from luggage, B) they often travel for free by checking themselves into the cargo hold, C) they hold informal competitions to see how hard they can throw bags at each other"
42. Say a Hail Mary, say
43. Saucer in the sky
44. Freestyle skiing category
45. Arrange dishes and utensils on, as a table
46. Monotonous routines
48. "So there you ___!"
49. Mannerly guy
50. It's even in tennis
51. Race postings
55. "A Houston airport dealt with persistent ___ the long wait to retrieve bags in what way? A) They arranged to have the airplanes drop the bags onto a large net as they came in for a landing, B) They hired competitive collegiate sprinters to run the bags to the terminal, C) They just made the walk to the baggage claim six times longer so people wouldn't be standing there waiting so long"
59. South-of-the border order
60. Politico Pawlenty
61. Assist
62. Legendary Colts quarterback Johnny
63. Flight deck calculation
64. Out of whack
65. "___ Wedding" (1990 Alan Alda film)
66. "Oh, brother!"
67. Nuisances

DOWN

1. Lava lamp lumps
2. Quran deity
3. Cop's ID
4. ___ 3 fish oil
5. "Peter Pan" dog
6. Advice to a young man from Horace Greely
7. "___ tells me!"
8. Popular plant "pet" brand
9. Soap actress Hall
10. Founder of the American Shakers
11. Belly button
12. Vowel-shaped support piece
13. Zabar and Manning
14. Deighton of spy-fi
22. Feeling of remorse
23. Kanye's kid
27. Hourly rate, say
28. "Oye Como Va" composer Puente
29. Tom yum cuisine
30. Radames' beloved, in opera
31. Christmas carol
32. "Raiders of the Lost Ark" slitherers
33. Trifling
34. "Shoo, critter!"
35. Make an effort
36. Closest buddies, in internet slang
37. Bobby with 270 goals
39. N.W.A's "Straight ___ Compton"
40. Peerage types
41. Placekicker's prop
46. Video that's often instant
47. Except if
48. "Nashville" director Robert
49. Future MBAs' exams
50. Law professor Hill
51. Tipping the scales
52. Uncool crowd
53. Comforter
54. Hearty winter dishes
55. Walking stick
56. Not put in
57. Gossip magazine topic
58. Letters meant to cause a rush
59. Bathing vessel

ACROSS

1. Pride letters before Q
5. "Of course…"
10. Clue weapon
14. Muchos meses
15. University of Nebraska campus site
16. Unsigned, as an article: Abbr.
17. See 23-Across
18. "This week, a costume company recalled a toy firefighter's hat, saying that it was a potential ___"
20. Caterer's container
21. Stitch up, as a wound
22. Suffix with song, slug, gab, or snooze
23. With 17- and 61-Across, "After responding to a life-saving call, paramedics in England returned to their ambulance and found a note on the ambulance saying ___"
27. Chauvinist
29. "___ better not…"
30. Period named for a monarch, perhaps
31. Pal of Pooh
32. Quarterback Brady
34. "That's what ___ said!"
35. Email command
36. "St. Louis residents are trying to solve the mystery of who keeps leaving ___ on an I-270 exit ramp"
40. Put six feet under, say
41. What the second letter in 1-Across stands for
42. Mauna ___ Observatory
43. 911 respondent, briefly
44. The "O" in SOS
45. "Diana" crooner Paul
48. iPhone program
49. With 58-Across, "Police in Wisconsin say they're on the hunt for a suspect who has been going around town ___"
54. Weary exhale
56. Pool division
57. ___ Speedwagon
58. See 49-Across
61. See 23-Across
62. Puerto ___
63. "Haystacks" painter
64. Tiny tunnelers
65. Chest-beating simians
66. Skin cream brand
67. Have a fling?

DOWN

1. Drink, as a kitten might do to milk
2. Cool, for surfers
3. Island east of Sumatra
4. "How naughty of you!"
5. Like some checking at the bank
6. Have ___ of one's own
7. Slow, in music
8. Michael of "Weekend Update"
9. "Like that's gonna happen!"
10. Level
11. Binging, say
12. Helpings of food
13. Möbius strip's lack
19. Mennen shaving brand
21. PCs once ran on it
24. Singing cowboy Gene
25. Soda brand that sounds like a type of sock
26. Vacuum cleaner brand named for its founder
28. Divine being
33. Business giant
34. Gatherer of intelligence
35. Nonstandard speech
36. Abandon the cause
37. Museum holding
38. Gambler's card game that sounds like an ancient Egyptian ruler
39. "Family Circus" cartoonist Bil
40. TV actress Arthur
44. Dos x cuatro
46. Yeah Yeah Yeahs singer
47. They may be accompanied by "ping!" sounds on phones
50. Astronaut John
51. Like many fancy estates
52. Schools like Cal Tech: Abbr.
53. Wind-borne silt
55. Old Pontiac models
58. Lilted syllable
59. Little bundle of trouble
60. Liverpool lav
61. Derby, e.g.

ACROSS

1. Comes down during winter
6. Reggaeton singer Don ___
10. Wound cover
14. Language of Carthage
15. "Move it! Move it!"
16. Dig it
17. "K-Tel was founded by a Canadian salesman named Phil Kives, who learned his trade hawking wares on a boardwalk. But before that, he had ___ as A) a Royal Mountie, B) a weasel trapper, C) a poutine cook"
19. Certain head of a middle eastern state
20. Cookie on a sundae
21. Go from green to red, often
22. Supports
26. Film critic Kael
28. Online troublemakers
29. Lift the curtain on
30. Christmastime hymn "___ Dei"
31. Some are bookmarked
32. Ripped muscles, perhaps
35. Grand affair
36. Sci-fi beam
37. Instruction line
38. New Deal monogram
39. Parimutuel proposition
40. Super Mario's brother
41. O'Neill's "The ___ Cometh"
43. Abandon on an isle
44. Politically left-leaning
46. Cries of sorrow
47. Embryo sac site
48. Atkins diet no-no
49. Religious ceremony
50. Governor who answered this puzzle's questions on April 7, 2018
56. Animal that may get caught in the headlights
57. Earsplitting
58. New ___ (India's capital)
59. Whirling water
60. Electrical units represented by omegas
61. Wheel turners

DOWN

1. Place to get a facial mask
2. Letter on a dreidel
3. "Imagine Peace" activist
4. Improv comic's asset
5. Fish groupings
6. Fairy tale villains
7. Austin Powers' "power"
8. Prior to this date
9. Steal from
10. Aussie lassie
11. "Which of these was a real K-Tel ___ album? A) '24 Dumb Ditties,' B) '38 Tuba Explosions,' C) '76 Tromboners'"
12. UFO driver
13. Swiss capital, to the Swiss
18. Goes off course
21. Regrets greatly
22. Workforce
23. Strongly recommended
24. "For all their kitchiness, K-Tel albums ___ to the history of American pop music in at least one significant way, namely A) the desk at which Michael Jackson wrote 'Beat It' had a leg balanced on six stacked K-Tel records, B) Dave Grohl of Nirvana says it was a K-Tel record that inspired his musical career, C) the CD and, thus, digital music was invented by a computer scientist who was upset that his vinyl copies of K-Tel's 'Summer Cruisin'' kept wearing out"
25. One of 78 in this puzzle
26. With 31-Down, "Wait Wait...Don't Tell Me!" host
27. Profess
29. Like some dough, or Jesus
31. See 26-Down
33. Brought forth, biblically
34. Plays with, as a dreidel
36. Eastern religious figure
37. Beyond a doubt
39. "What ___ you thinking?!"
40. Sensuous Brazilian dance
42. Crunchy veggie
43. Question ___
44. "Royals" singer
45. Like some of Harvard and Princeton's walls
46. Arrives
48. Ground bait for fish
50. "Love Don't Cost a Thing" singer, to fans
51. "Man, that's nice!"
52. Carrie Bradshaw wrote about it
53. Sick as a dog
54. Guevara the guerrilla
55. Belonging to that guy

ACROSS

1. Pagan god
5. Brief Vimeo selection
9. Deintensify, as thirst
14. Smoked salmon
15. Fifty cents per mile, e.g.
16. No-___ (something useless)
17. Prayer closer
18. Lob trajectories
19. Health plan giant
20. "In a Lightning Fill In The Blank quiz on April 21, 2018, Peter Sagal shared a story in which ___ in Indiana were unsure of what to do after…"
23. Bring to a close
24. Freudian topic
25. Uses a rod and reel, say
29. Courted romantically
31. Botch
33. Actress Amurri or Longoria
34. Lacking adornment
37. Get ready
38. "…a woman brought in ___…"
41. Central
42. Antique shop desk
43. Subject of a Keatsian ode
44. Animated stinker Le Pew
45. Show in or out
49. Make more profound
51. Deface
53. Big name in body spray
54. "…who'd gotten ___"
58. Fly like an eagle?
61. Horse's snack
62. Sports figures?
63. Split in two
64. Head or back complaint
65. Bonus, at work
66. Forest moon where Ewoks live
67. Hatchling's home
68. Do a great job, in internet slang

DOWN

1. When someone might be right back
2. "Blueberry Hill" singer Fats
3. Go to extremes with
4. Swimmer's area
5. Jenny of diet plans
6. Indication not to rush, in music
7. Result of a bite
8. One that might bite
9. "Doctor Zhivago" actor Omar
10. Loamy soil
11. Sharp, as a pupil
12. Barbie's ex
13. Pitcher's stat, for short
21. Sick of it all
22. Cause and ___
26. Deli sandwich
27. Like every other number
28. Stuff from a tree
30. Make by working
31. Country crooner Haggard
32. River that flows to the Caspian Sea
35. One of the Williams sisters
36. 'Vette roof option
37. Dad, slangily
38. Long-eared hopper
39. A, to Bach
40. 35-Down's milieu
41. "Your name is ___"
44. Eye, informally
46. Composer George Frideric ___
47. Semicircular seat in a park
48. Sailors' morning warning
50. City near Utah Lake
51. Exaggerated stories
52. Valuable holding
55. Bank negotiation
56. Taint, as with poison
57. "Klutzy me!"
58. Elle : France :: ___ : U.S.
59. Terribly pale
60. Getting up there

ACROSS

1. Fruits that might be dried
5. Be a bigmouth
9. Uneaten scrap
12. Best grade, perhaps
14. Rank below marquess
15. Victory letter
16. German wine valley
17. Certain choral singer
18. New Year's ___
19. "Florida police reviewing a man's dashboard camera for proof that another driver had cut him off found that proof, and also found footage of the man ___ three hours earlier"
22. Anti-toothache brand
23. "Another Brick in the ___" (Pink Floyd)
25. Wrestling bad guy
26. With 34-Across, "Portions of a 500-year-old Scottish castle were closed to the public this week after they were taken over by a ___"
30. Miss from Mexico: Abbr.
32. Designation for extra-wide shoes
33. Uvea locale
34. See 26-Across
37. TDs are worth six
40. Utilize
41. Soul legend Redding
45. "After getting in a fight with his mom when she canceled the family trip to Bali, a 12-year-old boy in Australia flew to Bali ___"
49. Envelope additions: Abbr.
51. Ship's pole
52. Eavesdropping distance
54. "This week, scientists in Singapore shocked the world by unveiling a pair of robots that can successfully assemble ___"
58. Highest (or lowest) blackjack card
59. Change of address, to a realtor
60. Home of the Rays
61. Frat T
62. Football club that plays at Old Trafford, briefly
63. Online sales, as it were
64. The Eiger, for one
65. Record label for soul legend Redding
66. Cain's nephew

DOWN

1. Fawcett of "Charlie's Angels"
2. Apple products
3. More smooth-talking
4. Southern American region
5. Snoopy's breed
6. Classic refrain syllables
7. Painting and sculpting, e.g.
8. Rorschach test shape
9. Amount in excess
10. Carousing
11. Souvenir shop purchase
13. Dos y cuatro
20. Thanksgiving mo.
21. Consistently defeat, in slang
24. Chemical used in soap-making
27. Rule, briefly
28. "___-haw!"
29. "Space" or "stat" start
31. "I coulda been a contender, I coulda been somebody, instead of ___, which is what I am" ("On the Waterfront" line)
35. Beast of burden
36. Twice, the first name of a member of the Ramones
37. Christiane Amanpour's network
38. Characteristic
39. Corporate reorganization
42. Having left a will
43. Cruel
44. Arachnoid zodiac sign
46. Exasperated feeling
47. "The Phantom of the Opera" author Gaston
48. Ceiling appliance
50. Great buys
53. Marriage or bar mitzvah
55. Gives weapons to
56. Achievement
57. Upper limb bone
58. Move ___ snail's pace

DOWN

1. Coats with goo, as a "Ghostbusters" ghost
2. Ms. Kidman
3. Words said after handing someone a gift
4. Pooch that went to Oz
5. New England fish
6. Might have, informally
7. Director Serkis
8. Person living near you
9. Battery elements?
10. Big show, for short
11. Patrol vehicle in the military
12. Dancers' outfits
13. Fully
21. Onetime TWA rival
22. Literary postscript
27. President Bartlet of "The West Wing"
29. Apple tablets
31. See 26-Across
32. Hebrew's first letter
34. Sana'a resident
37. Big name in chips
38. "Kiss Me Deadly" rocker
39. Pin for a formal accessory
40. Exclamation of delight
41. Viper to avoid
46. Book of lines
48. Leisurely, in musical scores
49. To an even greater degree
50. Waiting to bat
52. Bayou biter
54. Qualifying races
57. Tapper of CNN
58. Hightail it
59. Salon item
60. Dime prez

ACROSS

1. With 68-Across, "This week, a British artist unveiled a new painting she made using 300-year-old ___ ..."
5. Read hastily
9. Serbian scientist that an electric car company is named after
14. Plastic surgeon's job, for short
15. Orange plastic thing near roadwork
16. Soar
17. "Colors" rapper
18. Gernreich who invented the monokini
19. Holder of thread in a sewing kit
20. With 56-Across, "Minnesota police, arresting a man for a drug offense, were undeterred when the man handed them a ___"

23. New Haven student's nickname
24. Do some sums
25. Some computer printers
26. With 31-Down, tourist attraction at Agra
28. Become fixed
30. -dextrous starter
32. Decent lot size
33. Fork it over
35. MapQuest's former owner
36. Actress Diane
37. "Unsatisfied with pepper spray, a company in China is now selling women 'anti-pervert ___'"
41. Lacking moisture
42. "Mamma ___!" (ABBA musical)
43. Mitch McConnell's party, briefly
44. Takes a rest, in a way
45. Elongated fishes

47. Company that introduced the Hula Hoop and Super Ball
51. Class action org.?
52. Chain that sells vitamins
53. Home for one of the AL's Sox teams
55. Draper of Sterling Cooper & Partners
56. See 20-Across
60. Propose, as an idea
61. Actress Shawkat of "Arrested Development"
62. Kind of molding
63. "Donnie ___" (2001 cult film)
64. Mo. #9
65. Abbr. for a potpourri
66. Golf's ___ Cup
67. Teacher's favorites
68. After 1-Across, "..., recovered from a ___, as her material"

ACROSS

1. Polish port city
7. Decides one will
13. Apprentice, for instance
14. Act deferentially (to)
15. Hometown of 61-Across
16. Stephens who won the 2017 US Open
17. Some Taiwanese computers
18. Group cofounded by Helen Keller
20. Raised, as racehorses
21. Explorer Hernando
23. Places
25. "Swiftlets are fancy ___ birds in Southeast Asia. They're prized primarily for A) their saliva, used to make a very expensive gourmet soup, B) being the only birds known to lay square eggs, good for stacking, C) their feathers, which are super absorbent and used to make the first Swiffer mops"
30. Disguise
33. "Able was I ___ I saw Elba"
34. Pond growth
35. Sports org. in a 1976 merger
36. "We all know that the Queen of England loves her corgi dogs, but she also has a strong connection with some fancy birds. A) At any time, she can choose to wear a "living crown," which is a crested pigeon trained to sit on her head, B) By law she owns every swan in ___, C) Among her body guards is the Queen's own eagle regiment, a squad of 12 trained attack birds"
39. Org. with Red Wings and Blue Jackets
40. Dame Nellie of opera
42. Naruhito's title, for short
43. "Hey, you!"
44. "The capercaillie is the world's largest grouse. It has been filmed A) Doing a triple axel while skating across a frozen lake, B) Beating BBC natural historian David ___ in a fight, C) Eating an entire anteater, earning it the name anteater eater"
48. Israeli desert
49. "How Do I Live" singer Yearwood
53. Early fall month: Abbr.
55. Beano alternative
58. Either blank in David Bowie's "___ to ___"
59. Unwilling (to)
61. Skateboarder who answered this puzzle's questions about fancy birds
63. Say again
64. Goes over
65. "Midnight Train to Georgia" singer Knight
66. "Give a hoot, don't pollute" owl

DOWN

1. Chromosome components
2. Music appealing to an older generation, facetiously
3. Aretha Franklin's longtime label
4. Dir. from St. Louis to Milwaukee
5. "Sonic the Hedgehog" creator
6. McDonald's mogul Ray
7. "I guess so…"
8. Capitol Hill figure, casually
9. It's solid blue on a pool table
10. Astrological set of twelve
11. Answering machine prompt
12. Had a balance
13. Tie, as a shoe
15. Melancholy
19. It may be laid down
22. Finished
24. Joie de vivre
26. "___ tu" (Verdi aria)
27. Dissuade
28. Casual turndowns
29. Dreidel stakes
30. Bear with a soft bed
31. Be on the lookout for?
32. "Push It" hip-hop group
36. Gunshot sound
37. "Te ___" ("I love you," in Spanish)
38. "Now, where did ___ my keys?"
41. Visibly embarrassed
43. Tries to scam online, in a way
45. Fathers, Biblically
46. Fertility clinic cells
47. Aged, on one's head
50. Not quite legit
51. Chops down
52. Pose, as a question
53. "America's Puppet Master" Tony
54. Daredevil Knievel
56. Winter supper option
57. Affectionate sign-off
60. "For instance…"
62. Base figure, for short

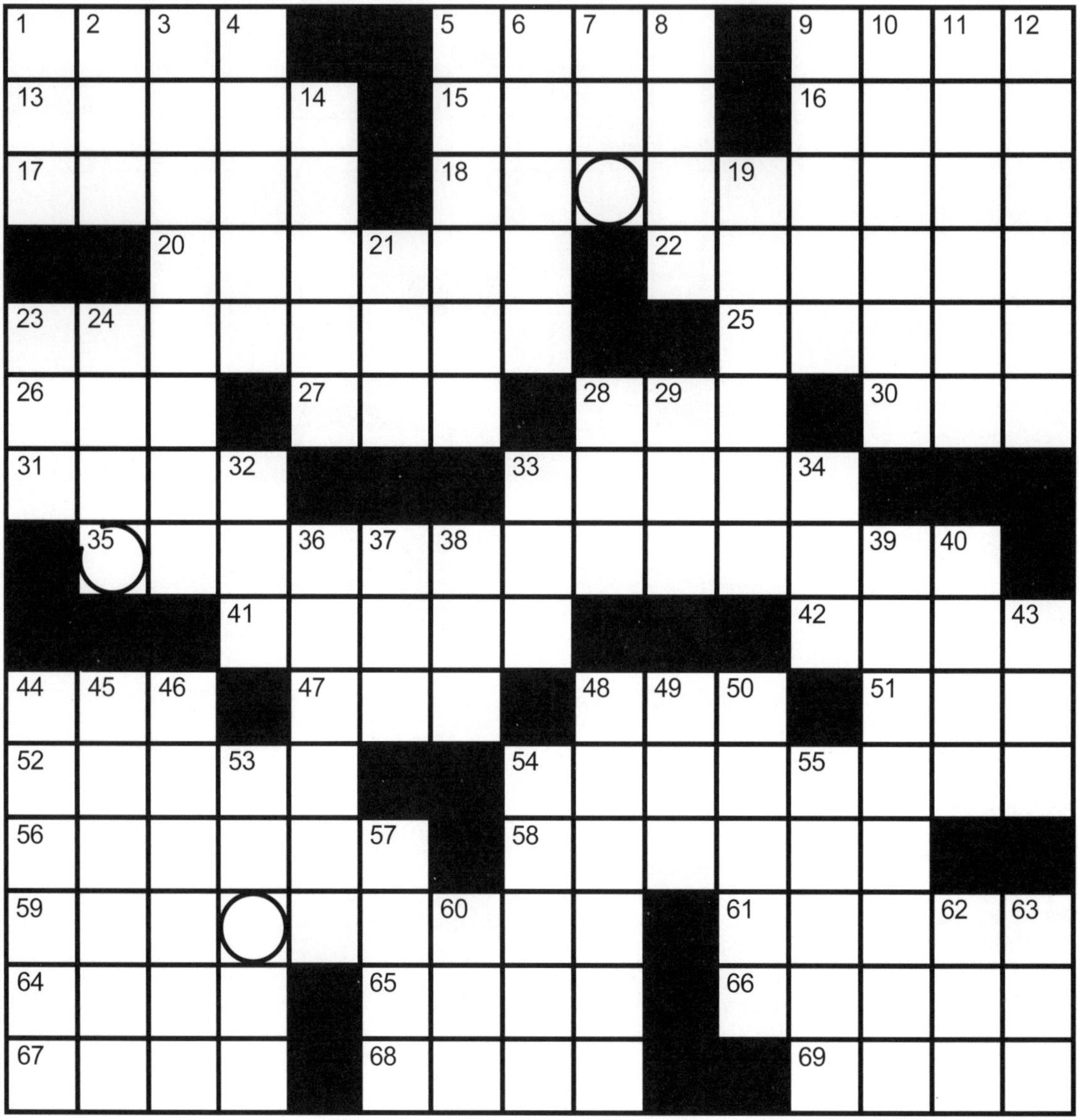

ACROSS

1. Santa ___ (Sonoma County seat)
5. "Octopussy" actress Adams
9. Regretted
13. Put into a book, perhaps
15. "___ sorry!" (words of apology)
16. About, in memos
17. Prefix meaning "great"
18. With 23-Across, "How Phish got its name has been a ___ among fans for decades. A fan suggested in Newsweek that, A) that's what band leader Trey Anastasio says instead of cursing—'aw, Phish,' B) it's an acronym meaning that psychedelic hypnotic instrumental sounds are happening, C) it's a take on the psh (ph) sound that comes out when you're filling a balloon to do nitrous oxide at a party in Vermont"
20. Break
22. No longer upset
23. See 18-Across
25. Elicit by reasoning
26. "Hip Hop is Dead" rapper
27. Fireman's chopping tool
28. Have
30. Matador's prize
31. Diagram with relatives
33. Rose-eating insect
35. "Phish has a fair amount of ___, including A) 'Morning Edition' host Steve Inskeep, who says he starts every day at 3 a.m. with, quote, 'a spliff and my Phish bootlegs,' B) musician Rob Zombie, who says he plays Phish music to 'go to my happy place,' C) actor Abe Vigoda, who played Detective Fish in the old 'Barney Miller' TV show, and once joined the band onstage dressed as a wombat when he was 92 years old"
41. Twisted look
42. Female fawns
44. Studio with a roaring mascot
47. Unit from a six-pack
48. ___-com (film with love interests)
51. Pvt.'s superior
52. Hawaiian hello or goodbye
54. Underwater explorer Fabien who answered this puzzle's questions about Phish on a "Not My Job" session on June 30, 2018
56. First three notes of the scale
58. Like citrus juices
59. "Lead singer Trey Anastasio was expelled from the University of Vermont ___ that he has never described in public, but according to Phish fans, it involved A) stealing a human heart and hand from a biology lab and sending them to a friend with a note reading 'heard you could use a hand,' B) getting a gig playing 'The Star-Spangled Banner' at a UV football game and keeping it going for 18 minutes, C) serving pot brownies at a dean's reception"
61. Phrase in some psalms
64. Skip
65. Soul singer Chaka or Mongol Empire founder Genghis
66. Madrid man
67. Bakery bread selections
68. Event with discounts
69. Determines, as a price

DOWN

1. 45 or 33 1/3, for a record: Abbr.
2. Singer Rita
3. Take a tour
4. Singer Lennox
5. Maltreat
6. Not to be missed
7. PC hookup
8. Where a sensei teaches
9. Pushed through a sieve, as potatoes
10. "Not so!"
11. Beethoven's Third Symphony
12. More skillful
14. Princess's headgear
19. Should it be that
21. Nickname for a cowboy
23. Certain NFL turnover: Abbr.
24. DEA informant
28. ___ out (choose not to receive, as an email newsletter)
29. Tot's perpetual question
32. Raised Chicago trains
33. It can be fresh or hot or thin or dead
34. Pops
36. Set up a tent
37. "It'd ___ shame…"
38. ___ Faire (LARPer's event, informally)
39. Heat shield's location
40. Sonic the Hedgehog owner
43. Letters before V
44. Totally gaga over
45. Blue
46. Title professor in a Mitch Albom best-seller
48. Notre Dame coaching legend Knute
49. "Mais ___!"
50. PC operating system
53. Track prelims
54. Erie or Kiel
55. Ceramic pieces
57. Ticks off
60. "Figured it out!"
62. Utter nonsense
63. PhD holders, e.g.

ACROSS

1. Chichen Itza inhabitant
6. Modern smoke, for short
10. Ibiza, por ejemplo
14. Back-of-the-mouth dangler
15. Some food fishes
16. It's guarded in soccer
17. "Just one week after a summit with President Trump, ___ is reportedly rebuilding a long-range missile site"
19. Polly, to Tom Sawyer
20. Digging
21. Puppy biter
22. 1963 Alfred Hitchcock film villains
23. "According to a new study, ___ use was linked to a rise in mental health problems in teens"
26. Of the Vatican
29. Roadside bombs, for short
30. Amazon assistant
31. Grain-like pasta
33. Some switch positions
37. Manage to obtain
38. "On Wednesday, the DNC said they would not let ___ cover any of the party's primary debates"
41. Pint at the pub, perhaps
42. Business bigwig
44. They may be dropped after a performance
45. Zac of "Neighbors"
47. "The Fountainhead" novelist Ayn
49. Citi Field mascot
50. "The fiancée of slain journalist Jamal Khashoggi called on President Trump to be tougher on ___"
55. Calamari
56. Contact by phone, in a way
57. It may be broken at the finish line
61. Trio for each team in an inning
62. "This week, the Department of Justice said it wouldn't challenge the approval of AT&T's merger with ___"
64. Empty, as a cupboard
65. Churn
66. Biblical character who had one whale of a time
67. "Grand" brand of ice cream
68. "Need You Tonight" rock band
69. Up and about

DOWN

1. City bond, briefly
2. Bard of ___ (Shakespeare sobriquet)
3. Gobi abode
4. Instrument for Charlie Parker
5. "I don't think so …"
6. Reason for a food recall
7. Jazz pianist Chick
8. Imagines utopically
9. Fed. property manager
10. Unsatisfactory parental explanation
11. Sister of T'Challa, in "Black Panther"
12. Hamilton of "Terminator" films
13. Carpenters and harvesters, e.g.
18. "Finger lickin' good" food establishment
22. Sleeping spot
24. "Frozen" snowman
25. Feline's "feed me," perhaps
26. Send for
27. Trebek of "Jeopardy!"
28. Former Reds manager Rose
31. It can result in rust
32. Event held in Cleveland in 2016, for short
34. "Charlotte's Web" setting
35. Drifting chunk of ice
36. Mailed (off)
39. Prefix for present and potent
40. 18-wheeler
43. Carnival rides?
46. Campus area with Greek houses
48. Put two and two together, say
50. Group of friends
51. "Back in the Saddle Again" singer Gene
52. Alternate song arrangement
53. Figure skating jumps
54. "One more thing," in chatspeak
55. Beverage brand with a lizard logo
58. "Frozen" princess
59. Mountaintop
60. Celtic tongue
62. The first "T" in TNT
63. Steely Dan album of 1977

ACROSS

1. "Tik Tok" singer
6. Regatta rowers
11. Airwaves regulator, briefly
14. Furry marine frolicker
15. Big name in thesauruses
16. Palindromic exclamation
17. With 22-Across, "I don't live at the pole where ___ " (first line of a "Wait Wait…" limerick heard on November 3, 2018)
19. Dorm leaders
20. Big galoot
21. Future flower
22. See 17-Across
24. Coffee additive, for some
26. Tie
28. Bring to mind
29. "Ah, Wilderness!" playwright Eugene
31. Weather, as a storm
33. Considered, as one's options
36. "Another thing I forgot to say," in a letter
37. "All those songs make my brain into ___ " (second line of the limerick)
40. "Forgot About ___ " (Grammy-winning rap song)
42. University of Iowa athlete
43. Rises up
46. Beantown ballpark
50. Soccer Hall of Famer Lalas
51. Muslim mystic
54. "Mambo King" Puente
55. "I have suffered the peril / of too many ___ " (third and fourth lines of the limerick)
57. Adjacent (to)
59. "Mambo No. 5" singer Bega
60. Beehive State athlete
61. "I went nuts from exposure to ___ " (final line of the limerick)
64. "___ Misérables"
65. Beginning
66. "Say cheese!"
67. Big name in home security
68. Gets close to
69. Western squad

DOWN

1. Beach Boys hit of 1988
2. It goes from Jamaica Center to the World Trade Center
3. Repress
4. "___ Just Not That into You"
5. Torah holders
6. News shouter of yore
7. Rousey of the UFC
8. Chicken alternative, in an existential question
9. Join with a blowtorch
10. Cooked slowly, in a way
11. Some iterative code parts
12. Ascribe (to)
13. Mollycoddles
18. Signal to stop
23. 12/24 or 12/31, e.g.
25. Ironic image on the logo of the Royal New Zealand Air Force
27. Ship on the bottom of the ocean
30. "Funeral in Berlin" author Deighton
32. Obsession
34. "This American Life" host Ira
35. Adhere closely (to)
37. Most harsh
38. Caustic cleaner
39. Time to give up?
40. Bram Stoker novel of 1897
41. In the family
44. Kitchen brand that looks like a failed tic-tac-toe line
45. "Get Low" rapper
47. "The Sixth Sense" star Bruce
48. Micronesia, mostly
49. "Get it?"
52. "The Odd Couple" neatnik
53. Fedora fabrics
56. Basic trig function
58. Recipe measurement amt.
62. Snowden's former employer, briefly
63. Angsty, as it were

8. Yukon maker
9. USPS option
10. Prefix with Christ or hero
11. Sauce made with basil and pine nuts
12. University in Atlanta
13. Attractive checking account feature
18. Tech whiz, as it were
19. Prominent physical feature of Obama
22. Glides lightly (over)
23. Vietnam's capital
24. ___ Mrs. (certain married couple)
25. As one
26. Unappetizing porridge
29. Macy's rival
30. Gambling authority John (anagram of CRANES)
32. Mic holder
34. Honshu hub
35. French red wine
36. One-named Guns N' Roses guitarist
39. Prime examples
41. Head off
44. Furthermore
45. Frog's home
46. Taron's "Rocketman" role
47. Be dishonest with
48. British mime show, for short
50. Like fillets
52. Clickable iPhone image
53. City on the Caspian
55. "I've heard better…"
56. "___ tu" (Verdi aria)
57. Indian baked bread
58. Mao ___-tung
59. "Kosher ___" (another book by 22-Across)

ACROSS

1. Group that answers questions on "Wait Wait…Don't Tell Me!"
6. Fish tank gunk
10. With the stroke of ___
14. St. Teresa's home
15. Big truck
16. Dory's fish friend
17. With 38- and 54-Across, title of a book by 22-Across that rap duo Run the Jewels correctly identified during a "Three Questions" quiz
20. Diary starter
21. ___ d' (headwaiter)
22. With 50-Across, rabbi (and friend of Michael Jackson and Donald Trump) who wrote 17-Across (he also wrote 59-Down)
26. Long-nosed fish
27. Santana classic "___ Como Va"
28. Egyptian temple area near Luxor
29. ___ Kringle
31. Grant-___ (government funding)
32. Otis Redding's genre
33. Rom-___ (films with meet cutes)
37. Python in "Spamalot"
38. See 17-Across
39. Exhibit backer?
40. One of four on a square
41. Cloud of gloom
42. Luxury handbag maker
43. Sews, as socks
45. Leftists, to Archie Bunker
46. Killer Mike's bandmate in Run the Jewels, whose name is a homonym for a type of vinyl record

49. Trailblazed
50. See 22-Across
51. Network (with)
53. U2 frontman
54. See 17-Across
60. Springfield bus driver
61. Small Chinese dog, informally
62. Wipe out
63. Hour before one
64. Dull impact sound
65. Nasal spray brand

DOWN

1. Surface for a mouse
2. "Sweet but Psycho" singer ___ Max
3. Trivial complaint
4. Yale Club member
5. Rent collector
6. Chemist's test
7. Glance suggestively

ACROSS

1. "Oklahoma!" bad guy
4. Tax prep pros
8. Long-plumed marsh bird
13. "Double Fantasy" singer Yoko
14. Garbage boat
15. Bakery enticement
16. "On Sunday, UConn advanced to their 12th straight ____ appearance in the women's NCAA tournament"
18. Farmer's market bags, often
19. Roadside accident indicator
20. "As baseball season opened this week, the Texas Rangers' Elvis Andrus used his new walkup music, '____'"
22. Capture again
24. ASPCA part: Abbr.
25. "My Country, ____ of Thee"
26. First lady?
27. ____ Sutra
30. "Paradise Lost" angel
32. Mythical mountain creature
34. Baha'i temple's nine-sided shape
36. "On Sunday, Patriots tight end ____ announced he was retiring from the NFL"
40. Dress style introduced by Sun Yat-sen
41. d'Urbervilles resident
43. Italian scooter brand
45. Little cut
47. Baba flavoring
48. Prescription drug, for short
49. Orbiter occupied continuously since 2000, for short
51. Villainous queen in "Titus Andronicus"
53. "Saying he wanted to celebrate his team's big win with his granddad, a soccer fan in ____ rushed to the graveyard to dig up his grandpa's skull"
57. Acid neutralizers
58. Doing too many drugs, in a way
59. "On Monday, Virginia beat ____ to win the men's NCAA basketball tournament"
61. MMA fighter Rousey
62. Ward off
63. Turn down for Watt?
64. Fort Knox bar
65. Mulligan, essentially
66. This answer's location, appropriately

DOWN

1. Son of Cersei, on "Game of Thrones"
2. Parent company of over 400 brands
3. Support financially, as a cause
4. Half ____ (coffee order)
5. "No ____!" ("I'm happy to help!")
6. Mar or lago makeup
7. Balkan natives
8. Swallows one's pride, hard
9. David of "Rhoda"
10. Spin around on an axis
11. Lagasse in the kitchen
12. To-do list items
14. Not looking good
17. Pirate's cry
21. "I'm happy to help!"
23. Cook with the stovetop and then the oven
28. Bovine bellows
29. Year, to Caesar
31. MIT part
33. Some computers
35. Similar (to)
37. Appearing astounded, in a way
38. Camper's combustible fuel
39. "I'm happy to help!"
42. Broke into little pieces
43. "Fosse/____" (2019 FX drama)
44. Barely beating (out)
46. "Blue Ribbon" beer brand
48. New Zealand natives
50. Instrument for Ravi Shankar
52. Wrestling surface
54. Ecto's opposite
55. "Party of Five" actress Campbell
56. Sent packing
60. One who might be in a queerplatonic relationship, for short

1	2	3	4	5	6	7			8	9	10	11	12	13
14								15						
16								17						
18						19					20			
		21		22	23			24	25	26				
27	28	29		30			31				32	33	34	
35		36		37				38						
39			40				41	42						
43					44	45				46				
47				48					49		50			
		51				52				53				
54	55	56			57	58				59		60	61	62
63		64	65				66	67						
68							69							
70							71							

ACROSS

1. GPS predecessor
8. SPAM company
14. Very attentive
15. Big name in cosmetics
16. "SPAM has played an important role in history since its invention during the Depression. For example, it's been credited with A) creating the modern vegetarian movement, B) growing the mold that became penicillin, C) the Russian ___ over Nazi Germany in World War II"
17. Bird whose consumption as a delicacy is often banned
18. Detailed atlas part
19. Common PC port
20. "For shame!"
21. Charged
24. "This feels great!"
27. Vim and vigor
30. "There have been many different kinds of SPAM over the years, including A) a kosher SPAM for the ___, B) a high-end SPAM made with caviar, C) SPAM for dogs, because dogs will not eat the human version"
35. Chunk of marble, e.g.
37. Donald who headed both the MLB and NHL Players Association
38. Vowel-rich farming refrain
39. Like aged paper, perhaps
41. Blog update source
43. Broadcasting
44. Fiery October birthstone
46. Bad spots for teenagers?
47. "As food preferences have shifted towards unprocessed food, the Hormel company, which makes SPAM, has had to come up with new ways of selling their canned meat with a shelf life of eternity. So which of these is a real slogan Hormel used to get people to keep buying SPAM? A) 'Because that bunker won't stock itself,' B) 'It's like meat with a ___,' C) 'Extruded means extra tasty'"
50. Immigrant's course, for short
51. Philippa of "Hamilton"
52. "Wait Wait ... Don't Tell Me!" host Peter
54. The NFL's Browns, on scoreboards
57. Like the rockets' glare, in song
59. "Rabbit ___" (1971 John Updike sequel)
63. Beatles hit with a four-minute coda
66. 70-Across actor who answered this puzzle's questions about SPAM
68. Like SPAM still sitting on one's plate
69. Weaver of myth
70. Show on which 66-Across plays Don Draper
71. Gets to

DOWN

1. Sitarist Shankar
2. See 55-Down
3. MLB semifinal series
4. Stand in the way of
5. Popular baijiu brand
6. Sheet music abbreviation
7. "Gangnam Style" singer
8. Like many teas drunk before bed
9. Choose (to)
10. Frat row letter
11. Shed, as feathers
12. Important parts of history
13. All skin and bones
15. Scouring pad brand
19. With 65-Down, Salt Lake City collegian
22. "This shouldn't be looked at on the job" letters
23. "___ kidding me?!"
25. Hurries, old-style
26. Mediterranean port city near Tel Aviv
27. Mind-based military campaign, briefly
28. Kagan on the Supreme Court
29. Pacific Ocean nation whose capital is Ngerulmud
31. Corrections on a slip of paper included in a book
32. Model and former volleyball star Gabrielle
33. Outward appearances
34. Sing like a lonely goatherd, say
36. Euphoric state
40. Nabisco favorite since 1912
42. It's no walk in the park
45. VA hospital concern
48. Dairy brand with a cow mascot
49. "The Lion, the Witch, and the Wardrobe" setting
53. "The Merry Widow" composer Franz
54. Fish used for bait
55. With 2-Down, "The Unbearable Lightness of Being" actress
56. Looked over carefully
58. Night, poetically
60. Pair for some kids
61. "Yeah ... not gonna happen"
62. Group led by Charles Xavier
64. Sticky situation
65. See 19-Down
66. Talk at length
67. Fine mine find

DOWN

1. Pilgrimage to Mecca
2. "The Time Machine" race
3. One with regrets
4. Personifies
5. GameCube successor
6. Coming to a close
7. One with an invitation
8. Luxury hotel name
9. Bathing spot
10. Highway entrances
11. City served by Taoyuan Airport
12. Contributes
13. Opera box
14. GameCube ancestor
21. Took turns, say
24. Minimum attendance figure
26. Chooses, with "for"
27. Second stringers
28. Windy City airport
29. Slipped up
30. Cast a spell on
31. Muse of love poetry
32. Protest type of the 1960s
33. BBQ bit
35. Finnish cell phones
38. Delta Tau Chi, e.g.
39. Legendary Indian diamond
41. Fictional substance in Vonnegut's "Cat's Cradle"
42. "Wait Wait…Don't Tell Me!" airer
44. Mountain goats
45. Insect with eyespots on its wings
47. They may be rotated on a car
48. Kitchen measurement, for short
49. Two-dimensional calculation
50. Deborah in "The King and I"
52. Solheim Cup org.
54. West Point letters
55. Fly in the face of
56. Häagen-Dazs alternative
58. Tic ___ (brand of breath mint)
60. %, briefly

ACROSS

1. "Let's get started!"
9. Amounts to
15. Metal used for foil
16. Japanese dish whose name means "eel bowl"
17. "On Tuesday, the Wall Street Journal reported that ___ was telling supporters he planned to run in 2020"
18. "This week, a doping scandal led to the world's number one ___ player being stripped of all his medals"
19. "___ Dreams of Sushi" (2011 documentary)
20. Group also known as Daesh
22. Architectural recesses
23. "Knock it off!"
25. Where the heart is, it's said
27. "On Monday, investigators said they found clear similarities between two crashes of 737 Max 8 planes made by ___"
30. "For the second year in a row, Finland was named the world's ___ country"
34. Long-range basketball shot
35. "Rats!"
36. BBQ bit
37. Beagle's floppy features
38. Vulpine beasts
39. "The Green Hornet" role for Bruce Lee
40. "What ___ the odds?"
41. Bothered a lot
42. Away from one's desk
43. "On Monday, Utah's Republican-led legislature passed a bill curbing a ___ expansion approved by voters in 2018"
45. "This week, it was revealed that some apps for the ___ may be recording users' screens without their knowledge"
46. Prototype version
47. Spelling of television
48. In a relationship
51. Long, as odds
53. In the altogether
57. "On Wednesday, U.K. lawmakers rejected a move to support a second referendum on ___"
59. "A woman shocked her friends when she sent out an invitation for her wedding despite the fact that her boyfriend had not yet ___"
61. Tennis great Williams
62. Settle in to one's couch, say
63. Astronomical distance that's about 19 trillion miles
64. Places to park your butts?

ACROSS

1. "Right this minute!"
5. Fuel economy stat
8. They're not fake news
13. Only
14. Felipe in both the Canadian and Caribbean Baseball Hall of Fame
16. Sneezing word
17. "There's a Christmas Eve tradition in Norway that feels oddly like ___. In it, A) people hide all the brooms in the house so witches can't steal them, B) people serve a treat called candy corn, but it's just raw corn dipped in sugar"
19. Has to have
20. Big name in bath salts
21. Indian region known for its tea
23. Sound all lovey-dovey
24. Cuts in half, say, in a way
26. Tenure ___
28. Corazón who was the first female president of the Philippines
31. "In Spain, ___ celebrate the season with a festive household feature, A) sensual Santa, a wax figurine of a sexy Santa that is said to bring fertility, B) pooping log, a hollow log with a face you feed nuts, onions, and fruits until it falls out a hole in the bottom"
34. "Some Nights" band
35. Map within a map
37. "I can do that for you…"
38. Hipster's rental
40. Backsplash components
42. Pork or beans, e.g.
43. Brightly lit areas
45. "Well, obviously!"
47. Versatile vehicle, briefly
48. "In the month of December, South African ___ are told the charming story of A) Kitty, king of the mews, the legendary cat of Jesus never mentioned in the Bible, B) Danny, the ghost of a boy whose grandma killed him for eating too many cookies"

50. A, E, I, O, or U, e.g.
52. Push aside rudely
53. Emulate a cat, perhaps
54. Long stretch of time
56. Head for the exits
58. Common housecat type
62. Stuck on, as an idea
64. "In ___, people attend Christmas Mass, but the twist is that A) churchgoers arrive on roller skates, B) they serve a lot of extra communion wine, and then they all go home drunk"
66. Last year before AD
67. Sicilian smoker
68. Wine made from honey
69. "You press the button, we do the rest" camera company
70. Collector's goal
71. "Dancing Queen" band (and an answer key to this puzzle's four questions, in order)

DOWN

1. Queens stadium namesake
2. Ivory or Coast, for two
3. "___ well that ends well…"
4. The only woman to serve as Speaker of the House
5. Gaping chasm
6. "Guilty" and "not guilty"
7. Heads for the exit
8. It's sent to stars
9. Crush, as a final
10. "Look at this!"
11. Common list heading
12. Merely average
15. Tacit
18. Yemeni neighbor
22. Provide weapons to
25. Refuses to perform
27. Sign of treble?
28. Insurance company with a spokesduck
29. Verb in "The Raven"
30. Removed from one's network, as on Facebook

31. One with priors, perhaps
32. Ham it up
33. Meal featuring the four questions
36. Periodic oscillation
39. Cashier's drawer
41. "Star Trek" role for Cho
44. Plug-in that stops unwanted content online
46. Unit of frequency
49. ___ v. Wade
51. Aftershock from an accident
53. Tubular pasta
54. Cuddly "Star Wars" creature
55. Prefix for vintners
57. Former soldiers, for short
59. With "the," familiar name for a big UK network
60. Spill the beans
61. When tripled, "you get the picture"
63. [We don't know the date yet]
65. Consume edibles

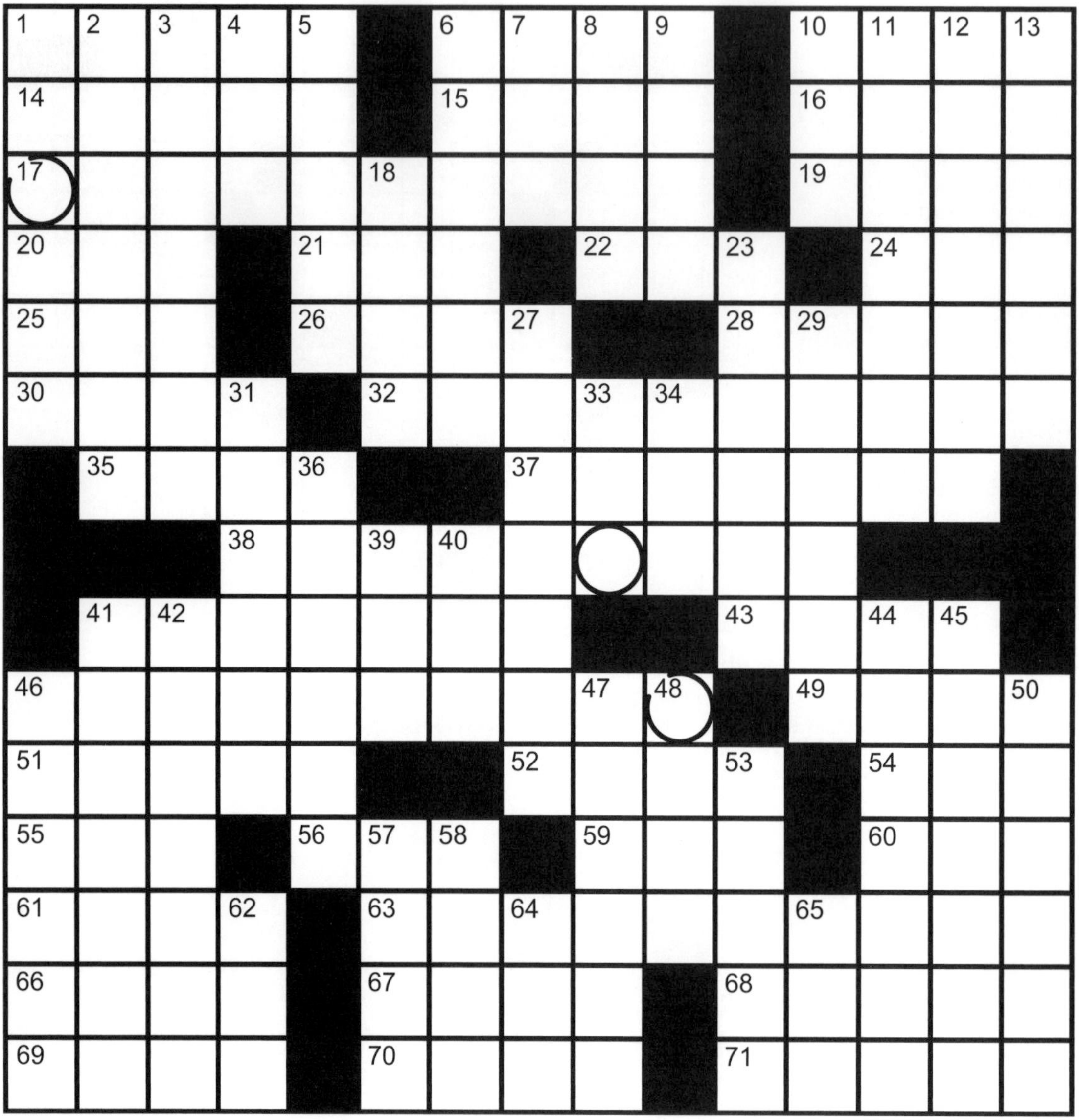

ACROSS

1. Direction indicator
6. Fleetwood Mac hit from "Tusk"
10. Cyrillic for USSR
14. "Gloria" singer Branigan
15. More than
16. Qatar University city
17. "After years of being the last rider over the ___ atop a racehorse ironically named Last Word, Alexander Fauvel visited the horse while eating a pickle and discovered that it had an extreme reaction. So Fauvel mounted the horse, took him out to the track, and showed him the pickle. Last Word took off like a rocket. 'We've been winning ever since,' said Fauvel. 'We get on that inside rail, I squeeze the reins in my right hand and the pickle in my left. Then I reach my pickle hand in front of his muzzle, and it's equine magic.'"
19. Square root of nueve
20. Map rtes.
21. Golfer's need
22. Key below the tilde, often
24. Play the ponies, e.g.
25. Unadon ingredient
26. Goes amiss
28. Deceive, in a way
30. Talk show physician
32. With 38-Across, "When a Perth, Australia, man glued his own butt to a six-foot wooden bar counter, he posted his predicament on Reddit—"So I'm kind of sitting here with a slab of jarrah attached to my butt cheeks watching ___ and waiting for the emergency services." After realizing the only chemicals he owned capable of divorcing his cheeks from his board were tucked away in the garage, he turned back to his Reddit feed to find 300 comments.

One jumped out at him. One commenter had read somewhere that the vinegar in pickle juice will break down an epoxy bond, and he had a jar of gherkins in reach. He was freed."
35. Gift bag goodies
37. Dig up
38. See 32-Across
41. California home to Warner Brothers
43. Cannabis plant
46. With 63-Across, "Estelle Schmidt of ___ always feared flying. Nothing could get her on a plane except her love for her great-grandfather, Marcel Muller. As long as anyone could remember, Marcel had provided the village's most pungent pickles. On his deathbed, he summoned 24-year-old Estelle and asked her to fly to Gibraltar to scatter his ashes. Then he bequeathed her his most beloved pickle, which marinates in a brine made with water in which Jesus washed his feet. Since Marcel's death, Estelle has carried this pickle. She knew...that the only way she could fly to Gibraltar was if she were clutching Marcel's pickle in her lap. But passengers on the small plane rioted over its noxious smell, so the Luxair flight attendant wrenched the green stink bomb from Estelle's hands and put it in the aircraft's minifridge. Even after being reunited with the pickle upon landing, Estelle sued the airline for mental anguish. The European Court of Justice heard the case. After witnessing Estelle's attachment to what one justice called the holy cucumber, the five judges ruled unanimously in her favor, legally naming it an emotional support pickle."

49. One minding his manor, perhaps
51. "Well, how about that!"
52. U.S. weather agcy.
54. Steamed Chinese bun
55. Cunning
56. Pine tree secretion
59. "It's cold in here!"
60. Devoid (of)
61. Adoption advocacy org.
63. See 46-Across
66. Puts on
67. Qatari head of state, for one
68. "Lux et Veritas" collegian
69. "Bye bye," in textspeak
70. BBQ skewer
71. Animal rounded up in a roundup

DOWN

1. Nobel of the Nobel Prize
2. NFL team soon to move to Vegas
3. Nearly disappears, as an inventory
4. "Either he goes ___ do!"
5. Use inefficiently, as time
6. Sherry classification
7. Social media profile picture, briefly
8. Monthly expense for many
9. Locale
10. Summertime Chicago clock setting
11. "Gentleman Jim" of boxing
12. Fastest feline
13. Sunday sermon speaker
18. Parsley, sage, rosemary, or thyme
23. Laundry additive, sometimes
27. Struggling with, as a homework question
29. Where Jaffa oranges are grown
31. Croatian capital
33. "Claws" network
34. Luau garland
36. Hawthorne title septet
39. "Leaving ___ Vegas"
40. "Your point being?"
41. Chuck E. Cheese playplace

42. Intense sobbing
44. "Might makes right" situation
45. Area near Lake Wobegon
46. Display hostility toward, as a kitten might
47. "Rules of Order" guy
48. Agricultural site
50. Brooklyn baseballer, once
53. "We Have the Meats" chain
57. Brewery options
58. Gas station fixture
62. Gallaudet University communication system, for short
64. Twelve, on a grandfather clock
65. Grain in Cheerios

ACROSS

1. Sings like Ella
6. High point
10. French Revolution figure killed by Corday
15. "The Legend of ___" (Nickelodeon show)
16. Amtrak track
17. In an unfriendly manner
18. Alaska or Hawaii, on many maps
19. Coastal bird
20. Nation south of Mount Everest
21. "For podcasts, we've got an ___" (first line of a "Wait Wait…" limerick heard on April 13, 2019)
22. "A Swedish voice sleep ___" (second line of the limerick)
24. Knighthood letters
25. "Oui" opposite
26. Romero of "Batman"
27. Pioneering visual kei band
29. Show appreciation toward, as a joke
31. Sassy and saucy
33. Captain of the Nautilus
34. Academic acknowledgment
36. Like some degrees
38. "Now HEMNES and ___" (third line of the limerick)
39. "Will help you stay ___" (fourth line of the limerick)
40. Turn in, as homework
42. Hard candy that can be chewed
46. Ackles of "Supernatural"
47. Page's "Juno" costar Michael
48. General in "The Last Jedi"
49. Big British reference book, for short
50. Calculus calculation
52. Improv comedy tenet
54. "Our podcast reads names from ___" (last line of the limerick)
56. Source of the names read on the podcast
58. "___ and Stimpy"
59. Bellini opera heroine
61. "Mi ___" ("My son," in Sonora)
62. Action figure since 1964
64. Pull, as heartstrings
65. Years in the Yucatan
66. Superstitious signs
67. Building level
68. Pride parade initials
69. Margin markings

DOWN

1. Taos activity
2. Andean birds of prey
3. Former late night TV host Hall
4. Turner of the Nationals
5. ACT cousin
6. Two-dimensional calculations
7. Vienna Circle philosopher Rudolf
8. Mosque feature
9. Monopoly util.
10. "Anaconda" rapper Nicki
11. Pitching staff leader
12. Eagerly unwrap
13. "The Heart of Dixie"
14. Aleve alternative
22. Place for some careful vetting?
23. Sandwich spread request
26. Halloween apple coating
28. Pink Floyd album with the songs "Dogs" and "Sheep"
30. Prepares for an extraction, perhaps
32. Happen again and again
35. Ambulance attendant, for short
37. Sports org. led by Rob Manfred
40. Go looking for
41. Be subjected to
42. "You oughta be employed!"
43. Luxury air travel choice
44. Office phone button
45. Blue state?
46. Shoulders and knees, but not heads or toes
47. Acknowledging academically
51. Taj ___
53. Actively encourage
55. Omnia vincit ___ (love conquers all)
57. Failed to win
60. Whichever
63. "I have some thoughts," briefly

ACROSS

1. Bounces off walls, in pool
7. Surveillance network, for short
11. Place to get a mani-pedi
14. Early newsgroup system
15. River of Spain that becomes a foreign currency if you change the second letter
16. Question of method
17. "___ was not originally invented to use on trees, but instead on … A) very well done steaks, B) enemy ships C), people"
19. Manchester United manager ___ Gunnar Solskjêr
20. End up with fewer points
21. Pick-six in the NFL, for short
22. Ditch, with "of"
24. Before, in poetry
25. ___-existing condition
26. Baseball legend nicknamed "Little Giant"
27. Factors in final grades, often
29. Type of herring
31. Show one's dimples, perhaps
33. Snatch
35. Swalwell who sought … nomination, briefly
37. Dangerous, in a way, as a winter road
38. "The ___, waged between two bands of 63-Across, ended when … A) they looked at each other and said, what the hell are we doing? We just got drunk, B) right before the battle, 14 different pairs of suspenders snapped at once, and the fallen pants prevented any fighting, C) both sides were scared off by a black bear"
43. "Right you ___!"
44. Shake alternative
45. Word in a negative phrase
46. Certain fed. operative
48. Funny actress of old Martha
50. Stranger than strange
54. Elegantly clad
56. Redbox rental
58. Person with a corner office
59. Edward Everett, for one
60. Info fudged with a fake ID
61. Something needed for your own sake?
62. 5, for some golf holes
63. "___ used to enjoy telling stories about fearsome creatures who lived in the woods and preyed on them. They included A) the ear lamprey, a creature that lived on human earwax, B) the Dungarvan hooter, a creature that pounded them into a gas and then inhaled them, C) the Tree Hugger, a leech-like beast that clamped onto trees and whined about rare birds"
66. Do something!
67. Radio knob
68. Continue, as in a boat
69. "Pay attention!"
70. Ophthalmic affliction
71. Impassioned, as a plea

DOWN

1. Veal piece
2. No longer on the sea
3. ___ Peanut Butter Cups
4. Never to be repeated
5. Just kinda fine
6. Unit in a flight?
7. 1/100th of a euro
8. Stephen Colbert's channel
9. Dramatic actor who doesn't do comedies
10. A, E, I, O, or U
11. Part of a beef slab
12. D.C. newsmagazine
13. Blown away
18. Dom Pedro's slain lover
23. Dress smartly, with "out"
25. Song of King David
26. Five-time Latin Grammy Award winner Anthony
28. Blast cause
30. Packing weight
32. Big Apple sch.
34. Be successful
36. Mass of bodies
38. It may be paper or plastic
39. Two-way weapons buildup
40. "Alice in Wonderland" soiree
41. Lanolin-based skin care brand
42. Indignation
47. Annual hoops event: Abbr.
49. Rim
51. Eave hanger in winter
52. Guess
53. "Crime ___ pay…"
55. Does origami, say
57. Vice ___
59. Brightly colored fish
60. Suitably qualified
61. Bug spray brand
64. Pre-Johnson prime minister
65. Tip receptacle

Page 6

```
BAYOUS GABS HAS
CHEESE HIRE ART
CINDER ADAM RIO
INFUN HINDER
GRIPE PALM UGLY
HEPATIC EASY
OVAL ROOM PSYCH
SUN SAMBOJA ALA
TEAMO IONA KNAR
ESPN AGAINST
BRIG AGED SWIPE
FEMALE VESPA
LET ELSA TINDER
ASH SLID ORIOLE
TEE TAPE WESTIN
```

Page 7

```
RUSSIA HUAWEI
ISLANDS RANWILD
NEODADA ESTELLE
GRE NOGUCHI TEA
VENEZUELA
ATE STIRS TCB
TRACE HOHOS
RESTRIP ASONANT
ATTORNEYGENERAL
CHER DWELT DIME
TAT TUITION TIO
ELECTIONDAY
ABSENT FASCIA
BETE OTERI HARD
BAER ROGER ESAU
ARRS STONE NENE
```

Page 8

```
OBAMA BAJA COPS
NAVAL AWOL ARLO
TWIRL HAUL SEAN
OLDS BARRYSBONG
BIOME EASES
BONANZA BATH
OMARR MOI TSO
HORSEBACKRIDING
ROC UPS MINOR
ROBE MESSAGE
GREEK MEDOC
NORDSTROMS OSLO
ASIF HERO ASCAP
TIKI AFAR STONE
SEAR WILY PUTIN
```

Page 9

```
OZAWA HONE UHOH
FORES IMOK NOLO
FREESODAREFILLS
ERA EDEN ROSIE
DORITOS SLANTED
SSN HOOPS
VEGA SUNUP PTA
FLOWNUPSIDEDOWN
WIT OSAKA ROOT
AVERY MCA
ANSWERS FILMING
MULAN GLEE NEO
ADUIAWARENESSAD
TENT OBOE SIETE
IRKS NEWT EXTOL
```

Page 10

```
VLOG ELLE HOPPY
CAPA LION ATRIA
RITZ EVAC TCELL
SCIENCEFAIR SEE
BUTA MCATS
PROFILEPICTURE
WIE FOIL KOREA
OXEN NEARS PIPS
REVUP NEUF ZOE
FLAVOREDBRACES
LANAI REDO
LIU DEFLATEGATE
OFAGE FINI NUMB
AFTER ENDE ARAB
NYETS LESS CANS
```

Page 12

```
ANIMAL ABEL FAM
PICARO SEXY ULT
EXULTS PACE LOO
EYES RESULTS
MASK MABEL BOOS
CHU ROTOR HOFFA
SAL ONYX AOL
BURGERKINGTOY
HEY INGA NAW
ABNER ATTEN EMO
TROU STEEL TASK
OURMEAL RHEA
NIM UTAH ADULTS
ETA RUSE INNOUT
DSL OPTS RATTED
```

Page 13

```
SHAW BARB POSER
OUCH EDIE EXTRA
THEACTOFSTAYING
TOO LOO GREG
IMP HOME PLESSY
KARAOKE EDEN
EGAN ARROW GAS
ANDGETTINGDRUNK
SAO PRADA ONTO
SPEX NOODGES
SCHISM FINN ASH
POET OBI DEW
INYOURUNDERWEAR
CAMUS MERC IAGO
ENATE PREK IRON
```

Page 14

```
OHOK TBSP LOAD
VERA PIETA ORCA
ALZHEIMERS BERN
MOURN FACEBOOK
NACL WAXY
YWCA HOC LUFFY
AHH AMENS ROLES
MEASLESOUTBREAK
STRUT STIRS ARI
SOFTG ETA ISNT
FARE SIGN
BASEBALL TIANA
AJAR HALLOFFAME
JAKE ATWAR ITEM
AXED MESS XOXO
```

Page 15

```
COROT DOWD BOP
AMELIA MONAE IKE
RECALL OPAHS AIR
TRAVELEVENWORSE
OTS ORI ATE
PATDOWNEACHOTHER
ORS IOS AGO
MCJOB DEMO JASON
LEI EEL OUR
BOMBSNIFFINGCATS
ETD ACE REI
EXTREMECUDDLING
TSA ADELE GOESON
IAN TIGHT EUGENE
MUD ITSI POSED
```

Page 16

```
ANKA JETE PAUL
LOEB BOXIN HIFI
ICEE RIANT LRON
CAPTAINMARVEL
ITS DEF YEGODS
ACTED OHM EMCEE
HOLEPROOF KIX
MRSCARLET
REV TERIYAKIS
BOISE SYS TONAL
INSITU SHE FLA
ASASCREENPLAY
JAVA HEATS DIBS
EVIL EDITS ACLU
BASS RENE STEP
```

Page 17

```
OGLE BURY LADE
TRIM ISEE EVER
HAVINGANAFFAIR
EVENED SAT
RESEW SITTINGIN
MADAM SNOOTY
ADA GOYA TIRE
HIDDENSWORDINIT
ONEI ANNA GPS
SALSAS RIANT
THECLOSET AROSE
LSU KNICKS
USEDASLINGSHOT
ZETA AERO HERE
ITSY NTSB ARTE
```

Page 18

```
CCCP CELLO PESOS
HOLA ARIEL OLIVE
IDOL PANHELLENIC
PETEBUTTIGIEG
SCHOOL GAYLE
NEVE TEX ELO
GIGANTICFIREBALL
AVEC LILA ASIA
MIKHAILGORBACHEV
EEK LGA PAIR
SOAMI TCBEAR
FAVORITEHOBBY
ELAINEBENES WOOD
MOIRA INTRO ENDE
OLMEC SUSAN DYER
```

Page 20

```
NAPS BRED THOSE
AREA OOZE EATER
SIRI MARC ALTER
ADULTBRACESFOR
OOP ALE
EVERYONE FRENCH
XOX PIN ALOHA
UTILS AND DATES
RELAP III URI
BREXIT OKSTUPID
EAR AMP
ENGLISHTICKLER
ITALO VOID EAVE
LOTOF PHEN EVES
KNOPF SOSO PANT
```

Page 21

```
EKE SGTMAJ NAB
TOAD INSANE EYE
HAVINGAPINT WEE
ELEGANT TUSKS
LADEN BAA HASH
SURVEILLANCE
WAIT ZIN ANGRY
OWN CAMERAS LAY
MADRE LAP MEGA
AREALCOUNTRY
NEXT LOX SHARK
CAROL LIVEDIN
EVA ASAJUMPROPE
WAR GELATI OPEL
END STAMEN TNT
```

Page 22

```
CROW MEDS AJAR
HERE ARMED ROJO
ARIA TOMEI EVAN
PUBLICSERVICE
SNITCH IDI
HEADLESSBODY
WAGYU REDO OHIO
IMO PROVERB MEG
FEAT ONIN LASSI
INTOPLESSBAR
LOL INCASE
EDITORINCHIEF
TYRA OWING EMIR
WEIL PLANE RENO
OPEL SASS SEEN
```

Page 24

```
SOLO GTO ALTARS
AVID ERA REEDIT
FACEBOOK KOMODO
ELK ADJ PREP
THEATERGOERS
ELMO NINER
RAOUL EZIO AHI
ATTRACTIONSOPEN
TET RYAN SPELT
GAITS EXPO
HICKENLOOPER
ANNA GAG GIL
SCORNS COLORADO
TUTTUT POM OVER
ERESTU ADS DEAD
```

Page 25

```
PBJS AMES BFLAT
LOOP HALO ILOSE
YOGA OXEN LOOKS
CRYINGCLOSET
LOEB ASH RED
TURKISH ERS
OCT TOTE BIPOD
ACHICKENCOSTUME
DIONE SNOB PEN
FLY LICKING
SKI ASP AILS
OTHERPLAYERS
WALLE IPOD MEAT
ERODE MARY ETCH
DRESS ELKS TATE
```

Page 26

```
AJAR MARE BILES
SECO IRIS ISERE
PEAT MEGA ARENA
PICKINGUPFARES
ACTS IRE
TIPS REALCOW
THOU FRAT ARI
GIANTPIZZASPILL
ANN ALAR WIRY
MAXIMUM NATO
GAL BAUM
SECURITYPRISON
CROAT ALPS EXEC
AGONY KALE MERE
MOLAR EWES INFO
```

Page 27

```
ROSSI SHAKY COW
ELLEN OUTIE OVA
FLACK PROWL MED
SAMOSA ZIPPERS
PROM SUD
THEHOTLOOK BYRD
RANAT DUBS FOR
ARCH GINSU RISE
MEL ESTE TALIA
SMOG THISSUMMER
SEA ESPN
PLUMBER FAUNAE
FUR ODORS CRACK
USE UNTIE ASIDE
ITS TAHOE NARCS
```

Page 28

```
ICET SLOP SAMBA
NOVA PITA OVOID
SPECIALTY CENTO
PIN BRA AIRER
OLIVE CANGETYOU
TONITE LOOT ELS
TGV MALT ANDES
INTROUBLE
THEDA IFSO WOW
RAM ZOOM WHATIF
INAGARTEN ETHER
SNORE APR ENE
ROUTE GINOBILIS
OLEAN ARTS ELEC
NOLTE GAZE DOSO
```

Page 29

```
I M P S   P A U L   S H O A T
B R A E   I N N O   A A N D E
M C C A R T N E Y   S L E E P
P U T   S H I N   D E F I L E
C B S T V   E D D A   A L E E
        A P T   E R R O L
B E A M   R U D E   B E E F S
T W O O W L S   D O I N G I T
W E L S H   U R D U   G O R Y
        H Y D R O   T I T
H A H A   I P S A   C H A N T
O P E N U P   E L L E   L I E
P A N T S   M O B Y D I C K S
E R N E S   A L U M   N O E L
S T A R R   N A M E   N A S A
```

Page 30

```
F I G   H O L M   O R A L B
A V A   A R E A   M I N E R
R I B   N C A R   A N G E R
S E L F D A N C I N G
I D E A S       N I S S A N
      T O P C A T   F E D S
A T A   M E I R   D O L L Y
M O M J E A N S F O R M E N
A R B O R   C O O P   A R C
S A L K   L O N G E R
S H E E N A   F U D G E
S U B L I M I N A L S
S C O T T   I S E E   T O T
H A N E S   P L A N   E V E
E M E R Y   S E N D   D E E
```

Page 31

```
B O S S Y   S P A M   M T S
G L A N C E   Y O R E   O R O
I N A H E A P   R E P S   D I S
S A M U E L   N U M   S H E E P
A R E   R I G U P   E L S A
A L O T   A R T   L A C T A I D
C Y N I C   I M P A L A   S T S
    N A P P E R C I S E
W P M   B E E G E E   E A S E S
E L A P S E D   F U N   R I C H
B A D E   S A P I D   T H E
S N O R E   W E B   C U S T O M
I N N   C O R E   T O S L E E P
T E N   O B E Y   A L T A R S
E R A   N I N A   B E S T S
```

Page 32

```
S L O P   S A R A   O B A M A
P A P A   P R O F   N O L A N
A L E S   O T T O   A P P L Y
M A R T I N S C O R S E S E
S W A R M S       T A S E
      I D O L S   Z I P C A R
C E L E B R I T I E S   H B O
A M O S   M O B   P E L T
I M O   B R O K E N B O N E S
N A T G E O   E X E R T
    A L T J   P E A K E D
W I L L I A M S H A T N E R
M I L L I   P O L E   O E N O
E N S U E   A V O W   E L I O
H E A P S   N E W S   S T E P
```

Page 34

```
H E A T S   P O B O Y   A M P
I G L O O   O M E G A   R U E
H A P P Y   M E A L P R I Z E
O D O M   D A N T E   A S A P
    A R I D       T R E K
O L D S U P E R S I Z E
H Y A T T   U T N E   S I P
N O D S   M I N D S   T I R E
O N E   S I S I   O R G A N
    S T A R C H Y T I N E S
S W A Y       E A T S
B L O C   R U B I K   T A R A
F O R K O U T O F   F R I E S
F O R   O B E S E   R A D I I
S P Y   H Y P E R   A M E N S
```

Page 35

```
  P U R E E   N A B   S N O W
M I N U E T   A I L   H O D A
R E A D O N   T W O L I T E R
M A G I C A L       E T O N
O L E     A H I   W E L S H
M A D E I N N E W     A P E
    M N O   L E S   U N U M
A M I C H E L I N S T A R
B R A T   O T C   I T A
A L I   H A M P S H I R E
N O M S G   I T E   M A G
  M E M O   W I S H I N G
D E V E L O P S   S L U G G O
O V A L   D I E   L A T H E S
W E L L   E A T   A B U T S
```

Page 36

```
  H E D G E S   C L A S S Y
  I V A N K A   H I D E H O
  S A M U E L G O L D W Y N
        D U L L Y
M M A   T O E   E N S
C A N B E P R E T T Y
S I N E       R T E S
    D A N G E R O U S
A S P S   C U P I D   T O O L
W H O   W H I S P E R   R U E
L A P S E   L O O   E L A T E
R U P E R T M U R D O C H
H O L I D A Y   T I E C L I P
I N A N E T   M Y H E R O
P A R E D   E S S E X
```

Page 37

```
A G E D   N I P U P   M O R E
L U X E   I N A N E   A W A Y
I C A N N U R S E   R E N E
A C C I D E N T A L L Y
S I T A R   I V Y   E T C H A
      L O G S   S C H O L A R
O E D   P O O P   H I D I N G
C V I I   U N D E R   D O D O
H I S B E D   A S I A   S Y N
R A C E W A Y   O S L O
E N O L A   E A T   E S P N U
    I N V A D E D S P A I N
C A R E   A G O R A   R U G S
O L A V   S E R I F   E L E E
T I M E   E R E C T   Y A L E
```

Page 38

```
M A D   D N A   G O B A L D
A L I   H E R   S A M U R A I
G A S M A I N   I M A S T U D
I N M Y B L O O D   R I S E S
  I D I G   D E F   N Y R O
E L S E   O B E   L U G
R O S A   R O D E O S   D R E
I N A R U S H   G O C L E A R
E E L   B U R S A R   I T I S
    T I C   A D M   G O N E
G I N O   H A G   O A H U
O H A R A   N O R D S T R O M
F A K E M U D   H E Y S I R I
O V E R P A Y   E L L   N E T
R E D O S E   A S A   G O T
```

Page 39

```
R A J   R A P   F I R S T
E M U   E W E   A M I G O
F A R T S A N D T O O T S
      O R O S C O
E V E R Y W H E R E   H E R D
N I L         S T A T U E
D E I S M   H A W A I I A N S
    T A C O T R U C K
S I G O U R N E Y   K U D O S
O V E R D O       E R E
B Y T E   C A U G H T F I R E
      I S A Y S O
B I R T H D A Y P A R T Y
I C A R E   I L E   G O O
S H E E P   N E D   E O N
```

Page 40

```
C S I   C L A C K   S E A M S
O H M   H A N O I   P O L Y P
C O P S I T T I N G I N T H E
K E E L   H E L D O N   M E W
T R A M   L Y E   A R E
D R I V E R S S E A T   N O D
Y E A     S T L O
E E L   H E R D I N G   A F T
    O R S O   N I H
P I C   T H E I R C A T T L E
E G O   H O N   T E E M
R U N   A G O R A E   A L G A
M A T I N G K A N G A R O O S
I N A N E   I M A G E   P E T
T A C K S   S A T Y R   E R A
```

Page 41

```
S L A P S   M R I   S T R A D
E A S E L   E O N   N E H R U
A M A T I   A N S   I N U S E
P R E T E N D E D T O B E
Y O U R   N I E C E   R A N T
A I L   S V E L T E R   R A H
K L E P T O   D Y A B L E
    S U I T C A S E S
G A Y   O A T   A J A
A N D C R A W L E D A L O N G
G A S H E D   O C E A N O
A S P   B A L L A R D   Q E D
T H E B A G G A G E C H U T E
H E A R   E B S E N   M I T A
A S K A   T E D   O N E D
```

Page 42

```
C H A N N E L   H A L A S
H D R E A D Y   L I N A G E
E L E A Z A R   S U G A R E D
C R I M E F I G H T I N G
B R I T   O N E   H A T E
R O B O T   E R E   S E T S
A D O   R A Y S   G U M S
    H E B E A T U P A
M A N E   K A T E   I M P
H E L D   T I X   R O B O T
S E L F   U R N   X E N A
C R I M E F I G H T I N G
A B S A L O M   A R R A Y E D
M I S S I S   T E A R O S E
S E A T S   S E N D U P S
```

Page 43

```
T A P E D   F B I   W R E C K
O C H E R   O R B   A I S L E
S T O L E F R O M   D A T E R
C O N   I A N   L E A R
A N E A R B Y C E M E T E R Y
    I D O   T I V O
P Y T H O N   A C M E   H U M
L A I D   Y O S H I   H O P E
Y O N   I M U S   C R O T C H
W O E S   U L T
T O T E S T T H E I R M E T H
A K I N   B U N   N W A
L I L T S   F O R G L U T E N
I N D I A   I M O   S T O R K
A G E N T   R B S   D A T E S
```

Page 44

```
M A M E   B R A S   B A M B I
A B U T   R A S P   I S A A C
R O S A   A T T A   S I S S Y
C U T S T H E I R N O S E S
E N D   W E D   S O N   R I G
L D O P A   M E E T   S A N E
I I I   J L O   I T E M
W H E N T H E Y U S E I T
M E A T   S I C   T O N
A L L Y   A L T A   N A P E S
E L F   I G A   T M I   A R K
T O S N O R T C O C A I N E
H O P O N   I R O C   F R E E
A D E L E   T U S H   R U S T
D O N O R   Y E T I   O P T S
```

Page 45

```
S M A R T S   L E S S   A H I
I A M T O O   A N T I   C O N
F R I E N D L Y D O G   R O T
T S A   Y O U   C H E E S E
E B B   A M T R A K T R A I N
D A L E   H A L   A G E S
R E D U X   N E S S   E R E
    S I X P A C K O F
B R A   E X I T   I D I O T
L O N E   T A J   C U R E
A P O L O G Y B E E R   T E X
H A M I L L   A X E   C A P
N B A   D A V I N C I C O D E
I L L   E D A M   E N A M O R
K E Y   R E N O   L A M E N T
```

Page 46

```
S L A T   K A P P A   D E B T
C U B E   E V I L S   A Q U A
A L E C   T I E U P   D U C K
R U T H E C A R T E R   I K E
    N O H   O R A C L E
M C D O N A L D   S P R I T S
A L E   M A R K E T A B L E
M A C E   I D O   B R I G
B I L L M U R R A Y   I S U
O M A H A N   E N E R V A T E
C R I S C O   A N I
C H E   H O R R O R C O M I C
H E W S   I N A N E   L I M O
A C A I   L O G A N   E C I G
O K R A   S T A N D   T E N S
```

Page 48

```
S C A N S   S O L   P E E L
P A T I O   E N E   O N L Y
A P O L I C E O F F I C E R
T S P   R O D   T E N A C E
    K E Y       L T S
C U T I E   A C I D C E L L
O P E D   P I A N O   M O O
U S E D H I S F I N G E R S
P E N   A G L E T   A N N E
S T Y L U S E S   U T T E R
      W E N   E S T
S T E N C H   A G E   O D E
T H E S H A P E O F A G U N
A O N E   C O O   U P E N D
B U Y S   K I N   L E E K S
```

Page 49

```
S T A M P   U R N S   T A S K
E R R O L   R E A P   A N N E
C A M P A I G N H A S H T A G
S P Y   I D E A   T I E G S
    A N Y       M E E T
C A M E L S H U M P I N G
C H O I R   P A R I S   E E L
B A R D   B A S I L   A W R Y
S I T   H A S T E   F L A M E
N A K E D M O L E R A T S
    A L E S       Z E N
L E T H E   O G R E   S H A
A D R U N K M A N A S L E E P
Z I O N   I O T A   U S A F B
E T T A   T E S T   P U N T S
```

Page 50

```
S K A G   S W A P   S P E D
H I R E   S E A L E   P E L E
E W A N   H E R O N   E R I C
I B I Z A   M O N A L I S A
    E A R L   F A C U L T Y
D S L   G E O S   N A N
R O O T S   W H A T I K N O W
O D O R   S P I E S   E C H O
P A P A J O H N S   D R A I N
    F A R   S O L E   A O K
S T E A M E D   P A L O
W I L L S H O W   P I Z Z A
I B E G   E D I T S   O I L Y
G E N A   A G R E E   N O S E
S T A R   D E E D   E N O S
```

```
EBBS  HARM  UPPED
MARE  ESAU  NEHRU
BROWNCOWS   DRIED
LEG UHF     KOOK
ELAPSE  MOT   FDR
MYNA   SIXTWELVE
   NEONS  AHEART
  HERHOMEWORK
ECOLAW    ASAMI
THESTAIRS   EDIT
SOD   INK  MARINE
   IOTA REN  ATE
PASTA  WASSTOLEN
EVICT  ALVA  BINS
PATHS  YIPS  INDY
```

```
MARC     CLAIR  TRE
BRIAN   TRICIA  REP
AMAJORROLEIN    UFO
USEON       TWAIN
CORNELIUS  JOHNNY
UNOS  SOFA    ITEM
SEE   FEW    LOSER
HAVERFORDCOLLEGE
 LORNE   INK    HIT
ASTI  OKLA    OUZO
CARSON   STEELYDAN
TRUTH    OLLAS
ITD   WORLDHISTORY
ORG   OBLADI  TENOR
NEE   WISPS    RATS
```

```
SAGAL     BONN  ALMA
OMANIS   ARCO   ROAM
JAPANESEBARBECUE
USS   DVR    ADONAIS
   FRETAT    INT
NATIONALENQUIRER
ORALS   BEAUS    ABA
TETE   FLANGE  BIOS
PSU    BOUND  AESOP
COMMERCIALBREAKS
   AIM   ADULTS
ADORNED  NAS    ASS
BACKGROUNDCHECKS
ETTU   LOSS   KOREAN
LEAP   YMCA   WARTS
```

```
EVER   SHEBA   AWAY
LINE   LYSOL   THOU
SACS   APPLE   WALL
   IHAVENOSHOT
INOT          ERIC
GLOWHOT  BLESSU2
ELMS   DALAI   TARP
ABA   DEMISEC   RSA
RENEE   MAI   AZTEC
   STAIRCASE
PASTOR       MASTER
EYEEXAM   SYSTOLE
PELE   ROBOT   ERIN
PALM   AVILA   DATE
ARS    TETON   HEW
```

```
TOES     PARED   WAH
ARDOR   AIOLI    ELY
HOUSEARREST     LSD
ITA   ALL      ZOCOR
TURTLEEGGS     NORA
INDO    LIE     OMAN
 DOOM   RAJAH   ENT
   NOTENOUGH
TCM   DEICE    TOAT
HOAR   EKE      SMEE
ERNO   DISCUSSING
JOHNI   ELP      RAG
UNO   MATHEMATICS
REO   UHAUL   RETRO
YTD   PINTO    TEEN
```

```
TCBY   PACK    LESS
RELO   ELHI   JOYCE
ETAL   RAUL   INERT
BEZOSISGOINGTO
ERE  MLK  BMX    OOH
KARMA  AMYS   SEGA
  ART   STU    LYES
BUYTRADERJOES
PISA   OJO      EEG
BLTS   IFSO   LSATS
SLR  TKO  NFL    KAT
YOUMAYALSOLIKE
BJORN   TOAT   OMEN
BOPIT   INTO   ABUT
BESS    VEEP   MOPS
```

```
SEW   LACEDUP    ODD
NAH   OILLESS    TEA
USEACROSSSTITCH
BYTE    MIA      COOL
   RESPECTMY
   SELA    ALMA
CHOICESINLIFE
EOE   ASSUAGE    FNC
THIS    ARM      MOLE
ANKA   GUESS    URAL
TSHIRT       REDDIT
   LOOKWEIRD
TOYOU   EEL    ALEXA
INERT   MEL    TENTS
CEASE   PDA    ORECK
```

```
JEDI   OOPS   JAFAR
IMAN   LUST   AWARE
BURNEDTHE     NAKED
   KID   AWL    KENO
TOBEACOW     OPERAS
RRR   MAR       SUE
ILES   LASH   NOBID
BOATYMCBOATFACE
ENDUE   LARD    FLAB
   LEE   TOO    THU
APPALL     JUGGLING
FLAM   OWE       RAM
RABBI   HOUSEDOWN
OILER   ENVY   ERNE
STORE   EGAD   NEWT
```

```
SAW     MACH   SCONE
ELI   BELLA   OHWOW
ALE   REPEL   FALSE
RUNOUTOFFOAM
CRESTS  SSN     PIGS
HERA    TSA      DEI
   KID   FEEL    LAX
INATRUMPTOWER
ODE   REPS       SUE
LEX   YDS       WORE
DATA   GTO    SOONER
   BREAKINGNEWS
ALERT   TAPIR    LAA
MONAE   EPODE    ORT
POEMS   RIDE     TMZ
```

```
DOH    WRAY      GONG
ENO   HUGE    CHOLER
LETJESUS      READTO
TAKETHEWHEEL
ACED      EAT    SMOG
STY  SMU  GEL     OHO
   FEMME     ADLIB
ORDERABURRITO
DIARY      BRAVE
ALF  ASH  NWA     ARK
MYTH    TUG      OPEN
   ATABANKDRIVE
AMBIEN   TACOBELL
PERKED   OPUS     COL
THRU     REPO     ENS
```

```
POTSDAM    SHUCKS
ISRAELI    HARARE
CHARLESTILLMAN
SAYIT   PHIL      EKE
   SPRITE       REC
TRIO    LINE     DANA
WATCHING        KIR
INSTANT      RESEAL
TDBANK      AIRBASE
   END   BBCRADIO
FEET    RARE     RYAN
IAN     YESIDO
ERR   AMID     CLEAN
SWEEPINGCHANGE
TIARAS     EARLIER
AGLETS     DREADED
```

```
AMISS   IPOD     MIL
AISLE   SUMO     ADA
ALTER   EMIR     NIB
   THEGREATACTOR
GOATEE       ALMA
ANT   SASS     BREST
GIST       CHASTE
   COUNTRYMUSIC
RISETO       SLOT
BIRTH   WOKE     OHO
ECOL        ELEVEN
RACECARDRIVER
ARK   OREO     DIYER
TUE   DINE     ECONO
EST   ADDS     STUTZ
```

```
ADAM    TYROS     HAD
REHAB   HEART     IDO
SNAKEPEOPLE      GOT
   ERIC        ORTH
HUGGINGPEOPLE
BLIP    ABE      PIES
RIDSOF  CROP      TAS
ONE    RUNNING   CPA
NEA   BRAE    SASHAY
CANE   DWI      METS
ORDERFASTFOOD
   SOHO       SICK
JOE   OUTOFCHEESE
AWE   DREWU    ORGAN
MLK   ESSEN     SOLD
```

```
BODE    DUMMY   APES
ICET    IREAD   LENO
FAMOUSAMOS      ERGO
ONE    ACNE    ORKIN
CAR   WSU    FORTUNE
ADIM     SLANT    PER
LATOYA      GREET
   STOREBOUGHT
TUGAT       PAIRED
SOB   BURQA    NOME
COOKIES  SAY     UAE
ALONG   PIPE      SIP
RAZA   LEEDANIELS
ELEC   OWNER    CREE
DARK   BEAST    USDA
```

```
MAGMA   ALFA   ARCH
USEON   NAIR   LALA
GIANTSTUFFEDTOY
SARA   AIDE   LOOSE
   LAY     PRUNES
THEIRSELFIES
ROAST  NILLY    POW
ELSA   MOVIE   SIDE
KEY   LIKEN   SNEER
   RIDINGAHORSE
HABEAS       JEW
ATEIN   ORCA   SPAR
USINGTHEIRPHONE
NENA   ANNA   AORTA
TAGS   NOTO   DETER
```

```
WEBS   PBS     CESTA
IMAC   AAH    DENNYS
MUCH   IRE    UNLOCK
PLOWEDRIGHT      ROI
SNAG   EKE      ORON
RIB   OTT    MOONING
POI    ATE       RYE
INTOTHEBUILDING
GOO   BSO       MOE
ANALIEN  DNA     PMS
GABE   BOO      DALI
ERR   IWASLOOKING
GIANNI  ALL     ICAN
ATMARS  GAG     NITA
PASTE   ERA     STEW
```

```
BOMBS   TESLA     OLD
ADIOS   ALIBI     NEO
HISNEIGHBORSCAT
TETE   PSIS    KEEPS
   UMA         FIX
POOPEDINHISYARD
ENRON   VIALS    TEE
NEON   CAPRA    BAIN
ANN    JONAS   EARNS
LOOKEDATHIMLIKE
NAS          SOL
DIJON   FOWL    CHAW
ITOWNEDTHEPLACE
VEE   ISITI    EULER
AMY   EPCOT    ABODE
```

```
GABON   GNC    DANIEL
LLAMA   OOH    ENABLE
OLDEN   WWI    INVAIN
BAGGAGEHANDLERS
SHEA    USE      OREL
   FIT   TREE     TAN
AMSTEL   BIT     OHIO
SECRETOFTHETRADE
PRAY    UFO    AERIAL
SET    RUTS      ARE
 GENT    ALL     ODDS
COMPLAINTSABOUT
TAMALE   TIM    SERVE
UNITAS   ETA    ASKEW
BETSYS   MAN    PESTS
```

```
LGBT   NATCH   ROPE
ANOS   OMAHA   ANON
PARK   FIREHAZARD
URN    MEND      FEST
PLEASEDONOT      PIG
YOUD    ERA       ROO
   TOM   SHE     SEND
JARSOFPICKLES
BURY   GAY       KEA
EMT    OUR      ANKA
APP   CLOGGINGALL
SIGH    LANE      REO
THETOILETS      HERE
RICO   MONET   ANTS
APES   PONDS   TOSS
```

```
SNOWS   OMAR    SCAB
PUNIC   GOGO    HOLE
ANOTHERJOB      EMIR
   OREO        RIPEN
SUCCORS     PAULINE
TROLLS       REVEAL
AGNUS   SITES    ABS
FETE   LASER    STEP
FDR   WAGER    LUIGI
   ICEMAN    MAROON
LIBERAL     LAMENTS
OVULE        CARB
RITE   JOHNKASICH
DEER   LOUD    DELHI
EDDY   OHMS    AXLES
```

Page 74

```
I D O L   C L I P   S L A K E
N O V A   R A T E   H O P E R
A M E N   A R C S   A E T N A
F I R E F I G H T E R S
E N D   E G O     F I S H E S
W O O E D   M U F F   E V A
    A U S T E R E   P R E P
H E R P E T R A C C O O N
M A I N   R O L L T O P
U R N   P E P E   U S H E R
D E E P E N   M A R   A X E
R E A L L Y S T O N E D
S W O O P   O A T S   O D D S
H A L V E   A C H E   P E R K
E N D O R   N E S T   S L A Y
```

Page 75

```
F I G S     B L A B   O R T
A P L U S   E A R L   V E E
R H I N E   A L T O   E V E
R O B B I N G A S T O R E
A N B E S O L       W A L L
H E E L   V E R Y A N G R Y
S R T A   E E E     E Y E
      B A D G E R
P T S   U S E     O T I S
B Y H I M S E L F   E N C S
S P A R     E A R S H O T
I K E A F U R N I T U R E
A C E   R E L O   T A M P A
T A U   M A N U   E T A I L
A L P   S T A X   E N O S
```

Page 76

```
S N O T   S C A N   T E S L A
L I P O   C O N E   E X C E L
I C E T   R U D I   S P O O L
M O N O P O L Y G E T O U T
E L I   A D D   H P S   T A J
S E T I N   A M B I   A C R E
    P A Y   A O L   L A D D
F L A M E T H R O W E R S
A R I D   M I A   G O P
S I T S   E E L S   W H A M O
P T A   G N C   C H I   D O N
O F J A I L F R E E C A R D
F L O A T   A L I A   O G E E
D A R K O   S E P T   M I S C
R Y D E R   P E T S   B O O K
```

Page 77

```
  G D A N S K   O P T S T O
L E A R N E R   K O W T O W
S A N D I E G O   S L O A N E
A C E R S   A C L U   B R E D
D E S O T O     A R E A S
    C A V E D W E L L I N G
M A S K   E R E   A L G A E
A B A   B R I T A I N   N H L
M E L B A   E M P   P S S T
A T T E N B O R O U G H
  N E G E V     T R I S H A
S E P T   G A S X   A S H E S
A V E R S E   T O N Y H A W K
R E P E A T   E X C E E D S
G L A D Y S   W O O D S Y
```

Page 78

```
R O S A   M A U D   R U E D
P R I N T   I M S O   I N R E
M A G N I   S U B J E C T O F
  H I A T U S   O V E R I T
I N T E R E S T   E D U C E
N A S   A X E   O W N   E A R
T R E E     A P H I D
C E L E B R I T Y F A N S
  S N E E R     D O E S
M G M   C A N   R O M   S G T
A L O H A   C O U S T E A U
D O R E M I   A C I D I C
F O R A P R A N K   O L O R D
O M I T   K H A N   S E N O R
R Y E S   S A L E   S E T S
```

Page 80

```
M A Y A N   E C I G   I S L A
U V U L A   C O D S   S H I N
N O R T H K O R E A   A U N T
I N T O   F L E A   B I R D S
    S O C I A L M E D I A
P A P A L   I E D S
A L E X A   O R Z O   O F F S
G E T   F O X N E W S
E X E C   M I C S   E F R O N
    R A N D     M R M E T
S A U D I A R A B I A
S Q U I D   T E X T   T A P E
O U T S   T I M E W A R N E R
B A R E   R O I L   J O N A S
E D Y S   I N X S   A W A K E
```

Page 81

```
K E S H A   C R E W S   F C C
O T T E R   R O G E T   O H O
K R I S K R I N G L E   R A S
O A F   S E E D   D W E L L S
M I L K   D R A W   E V O K E
O N E I L L   R I D E O U T
  W E I G H E D   P P S
S I N G L E C E L L S
D R E   H A W K E Y E
R E V O L T S   F E N W A Y
A L E X I   S U F I   T I T O
C A R O L S   N E X T   L O U
U T E   J I N G L E B E L L S
L E S   O N S E T   S M I L E
A D T   N E A R S   P O S S E
```

Page 82

```
P A N E L   A L G A   A P E N
A V I L A   S E M I   N E M O
D A T I N G S E C R E T S O F
    D E A R   M A I T R E
S H M U L E Y   G A R   O Y E
K A R N A K   K R I S S
I N A I D   S O U L   C O M S
M O N T Y   T H E   E A S E L
S I D E   P A L L   P R A D A
    D A R N S   P I N K O S
E L P   L E D   B O T E A C H
L I A I S E   B O N O
T E N C O M M A N D M E N T S
O T T O   P E K E   E R A S E
N O O N   T H U D   S I N E X
```

Page 83

```
J U D   C P A S   E G R E T
O N O   B A R G E   A R O M A
F I N A L F O U R   T O T E S
F L A R E   B A B Y S H A R K
R E T R A P   S O C   T I S
E V E   K A M A   U R I E L
Y E T I   N O N A G O N
R O B G R O N K O W S K I
  M A O S U I T   T E S S
V E S P A   S N I P   R U M
M E D   I S S   T A M O R A
A R G E N T I N A   B A S E S
O D I N G   T E X A S T E C H
R O N D A   A V E R T   N A E
I N G O T   R E D O   E N D
```

Page 84

```
R O A D M A P   H O R M E L
A L L E A R S   S E P H O R A
V I C T O R Y   O R T O L A N
I N S E T   U S B   T S K
    R A N A T   A H H
P E P   I S R A E L I A R M Y
S L A B   F E H R   E I E I O
Y E L L O W Y   R S S F E E D
O N A I R   O P A L   A C N E
P A U S E B U T T O N   E S L
    S O O   S A G A L
C L E   R E D   R E D U X
H E Y J U D E   J O N H A M M
U N E A T E N   A R I A D N E
M A D M E N   W E A R S O N
```

Page 86

```
H E R E W E G O   T O T A L S
A L U M I N U M   U N A D O N
J O E B I D E N   B R I D G E
J I R O   I S I S   A P S E S
    D O N T   H O M E
B O E I N G   H A P P I E S T
T H R E E   N E R T S   R I B
E A R S   F O X E S   K A T O
A R E   I R K E D   N O T I N
M E D I C A I D   I P H O N E
  B E T A   T O R I
T A K E N   S L I M   N U D E
B R E X I T   P R O P O S E D
S E R E N A   G E T C O M F Y
P A R S E C   A S H T R A Y S
```

Page 87

```
A S A P   M P G   F A C T S
S O L E   A L O U   A C H O O
H A L L O W E E N   N E E D S
E P S O M   A S S A M   C O O
    S A W S   T R A C K
A Q U I N O   F A M I L I E S
F U N   I N S E T   L E T M E
L O F T   T I L E S   F O O D
A T R I A   N O D U H   U T E
C H I L D R E N   L E T T E R
    E L B O W   P U R R
E O N   L E A V E   T A B B Y
W E D T O   V E N E Z U E L A
O N E B C   E T N A   M E A D
K O D A K   S E T   A B B A
```

Page 88

```
A R R O W   S A R A   C C C P
L A U R A   O V E R   D O H A
F I N I S H L I N E   T R E S
R D S   T E E   T A B   B E T
E E L   E R R S   L I E T O
D R O Z   B A T T L E S T A R
S W A G   U N E A R T H
    G A L A C T I C A
B U R B A N K   H E M P
H A G E L S D O R F   L O R D
I L L B E   N O A A   B A O
S L Y   S A P   B R R   R I D
S P C A   L U X E M B O U R G
A I R S   E M I R   Y A L I E
T T Y L   S P I T   S T E E R
```

Page 90

```
S C A T S   A C M E   M A R A T
K O R R A   R A I L   I C I L Y
I N S E T   E R N E   N E P A L
I D E A   P A N A C E A   O B E
N O N   C E S A R   X J A P A N
G R I N A T   P E R T   N E M O
S O U R C E   T E R M I N A L
    M A L M   C A L M
S U B M I T   G U M B A L L S
J E N S E N   C E R A   L E I A
O E D   L I M I T   Y E S A N D
I K E A   C A T A L O G   R E N
N O R M A   H I J O   G I J O E
T U G O N   A N O S   O M E N S
S T O R Y   L G B T   N O T E S
```

Page 91

```
C A R O M S   C C T V   S P A
U S E N E T   E B R O   H O W
T H E C H A I N S A W   O L E
L O S E   I N T   G E T R I D
E R E   P R E   M E L O T T
T E S T S   S H A D   G R I N
N A B   E R I C   I C Y
B A T T L E O F C A R I B O U
A R E   M A L T   N O R
G M A N   R A Y E   W E I R D
S P I F F Y   D V D   C E O
O R A T O R   A G E   R I C E
P A R   L U M B E R J A C K S
A C T   D I A L   S A I L O N
H E Y   S T Y E   A R D E N T
```

ABOUT THE AUTHORS

BRENDAN EMMETT QUIGLEY is a professional crossword constructor from Brookline, Massachusetts. When not writing puzzles, he plays a Remington in the Boston Typewriter Orchestra, who Peter Segal mistakenly introduced as the "Boston Typewriter Symphony" at a show in Chicago. Brendan lives with his two girls: his wife, Liz, and their daughter, Tabitha.

CHRISTOPHER ADAMS (he/him/his) is an independent puzzlemaker currently based in Iowa City, Iowa. He publishes his own puzzles at www.arctanxwords.blogspot.com, and has had puzzles published in a variety of mainstream outlets, including (but not limited to) the American Values Club Crossword, the *New York Times*, the *Wall Street Journal*, the *Los Angeles Times*, and *The Chronicle of Higher Education*. Christopher majored in mathematics at Cornell University, after which he spent a year teaching physics at Weill Cornell Medical College in Qatar. He later received his master's in mathematics from the University of Iowa.

BEN TAUSIG is editor of the American Values Club crossword, a subscription-based weekly puzzle, online at www.avxwords.com, which pays constructors equitably through a profit-sharing model and runs fun puzzles as well.

PETER SAGAL is the host of *Wait Wait . . . Don't Tell Me!* and the author of *The Book of Vice: Naughty Things and How to Do Them*, a series of essays about why we're compelled to behave badly. But, let's be honest, you probably recognize him as the snake charmer in the music video for Michael Jackson's "Remember the Time."